Conflict Resolution
in the Schools

Conflict Resolution in the Schools

A Manual for Educators

KATHRYN GIRARD
SUSAN J. KOCH

Sponsored by NID*R NATIONAL INSTITUTE FOR DISPUTE RESOLUTION
and the former NATIONAL ASSOCIATION OF MEDIATION IN EDUCATION

JOSSEY-BASS PUBLISHERS ▪ San Francisco

Substantial discounts on bulk quantities of Jossey-Bass books are available to corporations, professional associations, and other organizations. For details and discount information, contact the special sales department at Jossey-Bass Inc., Publishers (415) 433–1740; Fax (800) 605–2665.

For sales outside the United States, please contact your local Simon & Schuster International Office.

Manufactured in the United States of America on acid-free paper.

Library of Congress Cataloging-in-Publication Data
Girard, Kathryn. L.
     Conflict resolution in the schools : a manual for educators /
Kathryn Girard and Susan J. Koch. — 1st ed.
         p.   cm. — (The Jossey-Bass education series)
     "Sponsored by the National Institute for Dispute Resolution and the former National Association for Mediation in Education."
     Includes bibliographical references and index.
     ISBN 0-7879-0235-7
     1. School violence—United States—Prevention. 2. Conflict management—United States. 3. Classroom management—United States.
I. Koch, Susan J. II. National Institute for Dispute Resolution
(U.S.) III. National Association for Mediation in Education.
IV. Title. V. Series.
LB3013.3.G57   1996
371.7'82—dc20   96-10018
                                                                                          CIP

FIRST EDITION
HB Printing   10 9 8 7 6 5 4 3 2 1

CONTENTS

LIST OF EXERCISES

LIST OF EXHIBITS

PREFACE

Violence in our schools, our neighborhoods, and our communities has grown to an alarming level in the last few decades. Notions of personal responsibility and the common good have been overtaken by the strident assertion of individual rights, victimization, and punitive legal remedies. Court calendars are jammed, and formal legal procedures have proved unable to keep up with the load or to provide lasting, peaceable solutions.

Fortunately, alternative procedures have begun to take hold in schools and communities across the United States. Mediation and arbitration, long-time staples in labor relations, are now viewed as appropriate for resolving many types of conflicts. Neighborhood justice centers and local mediation services offer neighbors ways of handling interpersonal disputes. Many municipal and county courts now require litigants in certain types of cases to attempt mediated settlements. Family and divorce mediation has also emerged as a relatively inexpensive process that promotes more equitable resolutions. Conflict resolution programs in schools, particularly peer mediation models, have proliferated in elementary and secondary schools throughout the United States, and college campuses have experimented with ombudsperson positions, peer mediation, and staff training in conflict resolution.

As we stand poised at the beginning of the twenty-first century, two paths are clearly before us. Each has been emerging with greater intensity and definition over the past decade. One is the path of collaborative problem solving. This path strengthens our connections to one another as our common interests and the social and economic interdependence of our lives are revealed. Participation in cooperative and collaborative problem-solving approaches to conflict can support the development of broad and informed notions of self-interest, grounded in both a resonant acceptance of personal responsibility for our actions and a recognition of the importance of community. The other path before us is that of aggressive, adversarial confrontation aimed at producing "winners" and "losers." Along this path, narrow and isolated self-interest emerges. Focusing on strategies and positions over needs and interests leads to the abrogation of personal responsibility in favor of adjudicated determinations of rights, liability, and damages. Bringing conflict resolution skills into our educational system is one way curriculum supports the path of collaborative problem solving.

Accepting differences and increasing conflict resolution skills among all members of the school community are part of improving the climate in our schools. Such change is comprehensive, requiring that the formal and informal school curricula include teaching, training, experience, and practice in problem solving to resolve differences and disputes. Adults in the school community, who provide role models for young people, must lead the way. Therefore we have conceived this manual and guided its development to help adults in the school community understand conflict and the promise and methodologies of appropriate and effective conflict resolution strategies.

In our research and our experience we have found that there are a number of conflict resolution curricula focused on children. These consist of either peer mediation training programs, classroom mediation skill-building programs, classroom and schoolwide "peaceable school" programs, or violence prevention programs. However, there is very little in the way of teaching materials focused on teachers, principals, counselors, school psychologists, other school administrators, and policy makers. Working with an advisory group of educators, including deans of the schools of education of five colleges and universities and professionals from the field of conflict resolution, NIDR and NAME launched a joint project in 1993 called the Conflict Resolution in Teacher Education Project (CRTEP). The original purpose of this project was to develop, for those who work with pre-service and in-service educators, a curriculum suitable to preparing these educators to better understand the concepts and techniques of conflict resolution.

Eleven colleges and universities participated in the pilot project and were given the modules to review and use in their courses. Feedback from the twenty-six faculty involved in the pilot project and from the project's national advisory group has aided in the refinement of the materials.

The purpose of this manual is to support the incorporation of conflict resolution skills in the professional preparation of educators at the college, secondary, and elementary levels. Teachers, administrators, school counselors, and others who learn about conflict resolution through pre-service and in-service programs will be able to introduce improved problem-solving skills at every level of our nation's schools. In doing so, they will lay the foundation for a society of highly skilled peacemakers and a new century that embraces the values and behaviors that most rightly mark us as human.

The manual is designed for use by those who prepare elementary and secondary school teachers, administrators, and counselors, and by those who provide in-service training to these professionals. Course work and staff-development programs addressing classroom management, educational psychology, social studies curricula, health education, educational leadership, and communication skills are all potential homes for material on conflict resolution, and this manual has been designed to allow its use in such contexts. Separate courses and comprehensive staff development focused only on conflict resolution can also be built around the material presented here. Although these materials are not in themselves intended to provide the in-depth background and skills needed to function as a trained mediator or negotiator, they can help guide the acquisition of such training. Specialized training is essential for anyone who seeks to implement a program providing peer or professional mediation services or to use these skills effectively in his or her professional life.

Scope and Format of the Manual

Conflict Resolution in the Schools is organized into four curriculum modules plus a number of appendixes, including a glossary and some useful background material. Each module is organized to serve as a resource in the development of instructional sequences. Modules consist of the following materials:

- Learning outcomes shaping the selection of background material and exercises.

- A background essay covering the basic concepts addressed in the module.

- Exercises aimed at building understanding and skills. Each exercise identifies appropriate outcomes and includes notes on sequencing and conducting activities, based on prior implementation experiences.

Module 1, "The Nature of Conflict," examines the beliefs, attitudes, and behaviors related to conflict. It provides the basic concepts out of which an understanding of conflict and personal responses to it may arise.

Module 2, "The Concepts and Skills of Conflict Resolution," introduces the concepts and skills that form the foundation for resolving conflicts successfully. These include values that affect approaches to conflict resolution, listening and speaking skills, and ways of managing the anger that often accompanies conflict.

Module 3, "Alternative Dispute Resolution Processes," provides background information on negotiation, mediation, and consensus building, along with exercises aimed at building initial skills and understanding of these processes. This module aims to provide only an introductory understanding of the skills and processes employed in negotiation and mediation. Those interested in becoming mediators or in training others to serve as mediators are encouraged to seek out local or regional training programs. NAME, now at the National Institute for Dispute Resolution (NIDR), can be helpful in identifying available programs throughout the United States.

Module 4, "Applications for Conflict Resolution in Education," offers a sampling of the links between current educational goals, curricula, and concerns and the field of conflict resolution. It goes on to provide an overview of the various ways in which conflict resolution can be introduced in teacher education programs and in schools and classrooms, emphasizing the importance of careful decision making in bringing conflict resolution programs into education.

Additional materials supporting these modules have been included in the Appendixes. Appendix A provides a detailed glossary of terms. Appendix B summarizes guidelines for conducting role plays, including both the preparation and processing for role players and observers. Appendix C contains the situation and role descriptions for negotiation and mediation role plays. Appendix D provides an essay on power in conflict resolution. Appendix E lists recommended readings covering various aspects of conflict resolution. Appendix F provides outlines for including conflict resolution in course work and workshops.

An underlying assumption of these materials is that the concepts, techniques, and theoretical foundations of conflict resolution may be introduced to pre- and in-service educators in a variety of formats, from one-hour introductory lectures to three-unit courses, and in a variety of contexts, including classroom management, health education, counseling education, and social studies curricula. Therefore, while the four modules could be implemented in their entirety, we are assuming that most professionals using these materials will select those elements that best fit their particular setting, students, course context, and instructional goals. In that sense, these modules have been developed to supplement a curriculum-development process.

Another underlying assumption is that those interested in implementing conflict resolution in their courses will need training in conflict resolution. This is essential to ensure that there is coherence between what is taught, how it is taught, and the context in which it is taught. The lecture on the ineffectiveness of the lecture method is an old joke in education—and a painful one where incongruity between process and content still haunts the curriculum. It is essential to provide a context for teaching conflict resolution that offers appropriate modeling of the skills and principles in an educational setting. For this reason, as part of their curriculum planning, faculty should review their own skills and training in conflict resolution and the conflict resolution approaches used in their classrooms and departments.

Some Basic Definitions

While readers will find an in-depth explanation of mediation and negotiation processes and a full glossary of terms in the manual, it is useful to begin with a basic understanding of the general terms and approaches that frame the conflict resolution field. Here is a brief orientation to the types of semantic distinctions made in the field:

Alternative dispute resolution is a term embracing ways of settling conflicts other than by adjudication or force. This term, together with *conflict resolution,* as they are most typically used, encompass negotiation, conciliation, mediation, arbitration, and fact-finding. All these approaches, save negotiation, use a third party to help resolve conflicts. All but arbitration place the final resolution in the hands of the disputing parties.

Negotiation is generally understood as a voluntary process of problem solving or bargaining between disputing parties. The goal is to achieve an agreement that meets both parties' common concerns. Negotiations can be formal or informal.

Conciliation is generally understood as voluntary negotiation conducted with the help of a third party who brings disputing parties together to talk or carries information between them. Conciliation is usually an informal process.

Mediation refers to voluntary participation in a structured process where a neutral third party helps disputing parties identify their concerns and resolve their differences. Because it is a structured process, mediation is typically a formal process.

Fact-finding involves an investigation by a neutral third party, who then recommends a settlement. An ombudsperson often fills this role. His or her recommended settlements often go beyond the interests of the disputing parties, taking into account the institutional context and policies touched by the conflict.

Arbitration refers to voluntary or required participation in a formal process of presenting needs, interests, and positions before a neutral third party who then develops a binding or advisory settlement.

In these definitions, the term *formal* is used to signify those conflict resolution processes designated as required or optional steps to the adjudication of disputes. The term *informal* is used to refer to conflict resolution approaches used by friends, colleagues, or supervisors to resolve conflicts before they escalate. Conciliation and negotiation can be found in all social and work settings as part of informal conflict resolution processes.

For the purposes of this manual, we will be looking broadly at the nature of conflict and factors in its resolution. However, in terms of conflict resolution processes, we will focus on negotiation and mediation as the two that address the broadest set of skills and are most widely applied in schools.

Overview of the Conflict Resolution Field

Conflict resolution as a field has emerged out of several disciplines—sociology, social psychology, anthropology, law, criminal justice, political science, economics, education, communication, and even the biological sciences. Theories and research on interpersonal dynamics, group dynamics, culture and conflict, legal ethics, the role of our legal system, the cost of litigation, violence in the schools, and the psychology of anger have all contributed to our growing understanding of conflict and conflict resolution, including the costs associated with resolving conflicts and the effectiveness of various conflict resolution methods.

Early research on conflict reflects the impact of social psychology and anthropology on conflict resolution. Mary Parker Follett, a pioneer in conflict study, was the first to forward ideas of truly integrative solutions to conflict. Her thinking led beyond compromise to true collaboration to find solutions that meet underlying interests. The social psychologist Morton Deutsch, a major contributor to the development of conflict resolution theory, initiated his work in 1949 with a theoretical analysis and experimental study of the effects of cooperation and competition on group processes. Deutsch's theory of cooperation and competition identifies and delineates the benefits of structuring groups to be primitively interdependent. This landmark work served as a springboard for the cooperative learning movement. Deutsch and his colleagues at the International Center for Cooperation and Conflict Resolution have also conducted extensive research and theory development in the areas of conflict, controversy, and distributive justice. Deutsch's book *The Resolution of Conflict: Constructive and Restrictive Processes* (1973) remains one of the standard texts for the field.

Like Deutsch at Columbia, Roger Fisher and William Ury, writing from a law-school perspective with the Harvard Negotiation Project, provided another seminal work in conflict resolution: *Getting to Yes: Negotiating Agreement Without Giving In.* This book, first published in 1981, is considered the primer on the fundamentals of negotiation. It has been applied in such diverse settings as international diplomacy, business, divorce mediation, and interpersonal negotiation. Most recently, Bodine, Crawford, and Schrumpf (1994) have applied the principles of Fisher and Ury's negotiation theory in building upon William Kreidler's (1984) concept of the peaceable classroom. Their book, *Creating the Peaceable School,* examines applications of negotiation and peacemaking to the entire school environment.

In 1984, Robert Axelrod added another significant dimension to the field of conflict resolution with his book *The Evolution of Cooperation.* Framed around the well-known Prisoner's Dilemma game, Axelrod described a theory of cooperation that indicated the conditions and behaviors most likely to foster cooperation. Axelrod's work and the Prisoner's Dilemma concept continue to be important foundations for conflict resolution teaching and research.

Another foundation of conflict resolution theory is communication. Communication studies have contributed significantly to the advancement of conflict resolution theory and practice through the analysis of patterns of listening, speaking, and nonverbal communication. One of the most widely used college texts in conflict resolution courses is *Interpersonal Conflict,* written by Hocker and Wilmot (1991), both professors in communications studies.

As the multicultural nature of our society and its communities becomes increasingly evident and complex, work in intercultural conflict and gender studies, emerging from the fields of anthropology and sociology, is gaining prominence. The interaction between intercultural studies and conflict resolution addresses the premise that there are differences in how people experience conflict and various conflict resolution processes. Those differences are explained, at least in part, by race, class, ethnicity, gender, age, religion, physical abilities, sexual orientation, and life experience. Research conducted at the University of Victoria's Institute for Dispute Resolution confirms that culture, broadly defined as including all the elements listed above, plays a significant role in conflict and its resolution, even within specific cultural groups.

Exploring the implications of differences in how people experience conflict is a major component of conflict resolution study. The work in intercultural conflict and gender studies conducted by sociologists, anthropologists, and educators has been essential. Michelle LeBaron Duryea and Catherine Van Nostrand both look at conflict from the standpoint of difference, Duryea in *Conflict and Culture* (1992) and Van Nostrand in *Gender and Responsible Leadership* (1993). Early work in the field of gender studies by Carol Gilligan, professor of education at Harvard University, addresses the themes of "voice" (how people think and communicate) and "place" (the social structures and cultures in which communication occurs). Both of these concepts have been widely applied to understanding the unfolding of conflict. Additionally, Gilligan's identification of the differing focuses of adolescent boys and girls—the "care voice," emphasizing connection and relationships, versus the "justice voice," emphasizing rules and fairness—has prompted a review of mediation and negotiation processes for gender bias and has sparked research on possible links between mediator gender and mediation style and effectiveness.

Events and movements outside the university have influenced the development of conflict resolution as a field of study and affected the application of conflict resolution methods throughout our society. Social justice movements, grassroots initiatives, and alternatives within established institutions have all contributed to the development of conflict resolution theories and research. More importantly, however, events and movements outside the university have served to reflect the urgency of the subject and its place within our social fabric. The events of the 1990s have dramatically shown this. Political, social, and economic changes in Central and Eastern Europe, for example, have prompted requests for training in conflict resolution within a framework of education in the practices and principles of democracy, and they have underscored the central importance of alternative dispute resolution processes to our own democratic ideals and society.

In many respects, current conflict resolution programs can be seen as an outgrowth of those democratic ideals. The decades of the sixties and seventies encompassed a period of social unrest and action. Protests and confrontations related to social issues—sex, race, war, and poverty—characterized the period, as did the emergence of alternatives to established institutions—alternative schools, alternative technology, food co-ops, land trusts, communes. These protests, sparked by social injustice and a search for more humane and equitable approaches to educating people, growing food, sharing resources, and living in communities, fed into the development of community-based mediation. The end of the 1970s saw the establishment of neighborhood justice centers in at least six major cities. It is estimated that there are over four hundred of these centers today. In 1983, funded by the Ford Foundation, the Hewlett Foundation, and the MacArthur Foundation, the National Institute for Dispute Resolution (NIDR) was founded to promote the development of fair, effective, and efficient conflict resolution processes and programs. Over the course of its thirteen years, the NIDR has contributed to and recorded the growth of conflict resolution in courts, schools, state and local government, and communities.

Conflict Resolution in Education

Conflict resolution in the schools also emerged out of the social justice concerns of the 1960s and 1970s. While some groups, such as the Quakers, had long supported the teaching of problem solving and peacemaking to young children, a broad spectrum of religious and peace activists adopted this cause in the mid to late 1970s, and teachers began incorporating dispute resolution instruction into their curricula. In the early 1980s, Educators for Social Responsibility organized a national association that took as its central question the examination of how students could best learn alternative ways to deal with conflict. The Children's Creative Response to Conflict, the Community Boards Program, and the Peace Education Foundation led the development of the field of conflict resolution with their efforts in elementary schools.

Another concurrent development was the inclusion of law-related education in the social studies curriculum. Through this new curriculum component, students took on larger roles in instruction and classroom governance and gained a better understanding of dispute resolution mechanisms in our society. The growth of conflict resolution instruction and programs in the schools and the expansion of mediation and other alternative dispute resolution services in other sectors led to a joint meeting of educators and mediators in 1984 to consider how best to lay a foundation for teaching conflict resolution skills in the schools. A network and clearinghouse for information and training, the National Association for Mediation in Education (NAME), was formed and has been active ever since. In 1984, approximately fifty school-based conflict resolution programs existed in the United States. Eleven years later, NAME and NIDR estimate that there are well over five thousand.

From the beginning, the broadest goal of conflict resolution programs in the schools has been to teach better problem-solving strategies and decision-making skills. These are life skills that enhance interpersonal relationships, provide the necessary tools for building a climate within a school that is more cooperative and conducive to learning, and offer a framework for handling differences in ways that may lead to improved communication, greater understanding, and less fear. Through law-related education, conflict resolution approaches to classroom management, and school-wide peer mediation programs, students have the opportunity to strengthen their self-esteem, learn to appreciate diversity, improve their communications and analytical skills, and avoid disciplinary problems. Schools as a whole may benefit as these programs support staff and parents' abilities and willingness to cooperate and solve students' problems. Research on conflict resolution programs in the schools, while limited, does suggest that they have helped decrease violence and fighting, reduce name-calling and put-downs, decrease the number of suspensions, increase the self-esteem and self-respect of peer mediators, enable staff to deal more effectively with conflicts, and improve the school climate.

Conclusion

To recap, the material in this manual is designed to provide a background in the concepts and techniques of conflict resolution and to promote education in conflict resolution as part of the professional development of all educators. Educators and students share a responsibility for creating a school community where everyone feels safe, is valued, and can learn. By modeling and teaching the ideas and ideals of conflict resolution in pre-service and in-service education, we can contribute to the reduction of violence and the creation of peaceable classrooms for future generations.

References

Axelrod, R. M. (1984). *The evolution of cooperation.* New York: Basic Books.

Bodine, R. J., Crawford, D., & Schrumpf, F. (1994). *Creating the peaceable school.* Champaign, IL: Research Press.

Deutsch, M. (1973). *The resolution of conflict: Constructive and restrictive processes.* New Haven, CT: Yale University Press.

Duryea, M. L. (1992). *Conflict and culture.* Canada: UVIC Institute for Dispute Resolution.

Fisher, R., & Ury, W. (1981). *Getting to yes: Negotiating agreement without giving in.* Boston: Houghton Mifflin.

Hocker, J., & Wilmot, W. (1991). *Interpersonal conflict* (3rd ed.). Dubuque, IA: W. C. Brown.

Kreidler, W. (1984). *Creative conflict resolution: More than 200 activities for keeping peace in the classroom.* Glenview, IL: Scott, Foresman.

Van Nostrand, C. H. (1993). *Gender and responsible leadership.* Newbury Park, CA: Sage.

Editors' Acknowledgments _____

We feel considerable gratitude to our authors, Dr. Kathryn Girard and Dr. Susan Koch, for translating our vision—and the dedicated work of our advisory committee—into a reality. Dr. Girard and Dr. Koch have developed a curriculum that offers a significant contribution to the field of conflict resolution in education, and we hope it serves you well.

Annette Townley   *Santa Rosa, Calif.*
Judy Filner   *Washington, D.C.*
                                                  April 1996

Authors' Acknowledgments _____

Many experts in conflict resolution, education, and higher education contributed their expertise and ideas about how teacher education faculty could be supported in introducing conflict resolution into the professional preparation curriculum. We thank the following individuals and their institutions for their assistance: Morton Deutsch, Columbia Teachers College; Willis Hawley, University of Maryland; Frank Murray, University of Delaware; Elaine Witty, Norfolk State University; Wayne Benenson, Illinois State University; Dale Boatright and Ruth Wattenberg, American Federation of Teachers; Mary Dilworth, American Association for Colleges of Teacher Education; Carl Grant, University of Wisconsin; Cherylle and Lynn Malarz Moffet, Association for Supervision and Curriculum Development; Nancy Perry, Maine Department of Education; Virgil Peterson, West Virginia University.

Our work was enhanced by Ellen Raider, Columbia Teacher's College; Lee Richmond, Loyola College; Barbara Sarkis, AETNA Life Insurance Corporation; and Thomas Switzer, University of Northern Iowa. They all generously served as reviewers as materials were developed. Lee provided additional help by piloting materials in the summer of 1994. Ray Leal and Pamela Moore also offered important and helpful perspectives and ideas during the early development of materials, as did Donna Crawford, whose extensive and valuable suggestions we very much appreciate.

We also want to acknowledge the important contribution made by the faculty who piloted conflict resolution material in their courses as part of the Conflict Resolution in Teacher Education Project. In particular, we want to thank the following faculty for their valuable written comments on the materials and their experiences: Donna Allen, Emporia State University; Dianne Ashby and Margaret Shaw-Baker, Illinois State University; Terri Boggess, St. Mary's University; Allen Henderson, Texas Wesleyan University; and Marina Piscolish, University of Delaware.

Judith Filner, program director at NIDR, recognized the need for and potential of the project and then made it happen. Annette Townley worked with us through every round of revision, providing us with many of NAME's resources. We drew on her thinking and materials throughout, but especially on the subjects of cultural sensitivity and the application of conflict resolution in schools, historically and now. She deserves our very special appreciation for so generously sharing her knowledge and understanding of the field.

Kathryn Girard   *Pasadena, Calif.*
Susan J. Koch   *Cedar Falls, Idaho*
                                                        April 1996

THE AUTHORS

Kathryn Girard is based in Pasadena, California, where she runs a private consulting practice in educational program design and evaluation, specializing in conflict resolution and community building initiatives. She designs and conducts local, regional, and national research and training programs.

Girard has a master's and doctorate in curriculum development from the University of Massachusetts, Amherst. Trained as a mediator in 1984, Girard has mediated community, university, and court-referred disputes. She was a participant in the founding conference for the National Association for Mediation in Education.

As codirector of the Women's Equity Program at the University of Massachusetts and director of the research center and vice president for administration at Pacific Oaks College, Girard acquired extensive experience on the integration of conflict resolution programs into colleges and universities. Her publications include *Peaceful Persuasions,* which addresses mediation in higher education, and "Preparing Teachers for Conflict Resolution in the Schools," an overview of the field.

Susan J. Koch is an associate professor of health education at the University of Northern Iowa, where she cofounded and codirected the Conflict Resolution in Education Program, a professional preparation program for teachers, counselors, and school administrators. Koch helped design and implement the university's interdisciplinary Certificate Program in Conflict Resolution.

Koch holds an undergraduate degree in health education from Dakota State University and a master's degree in health education and doctorate in curriculum development from the University of Northern Iowa. Her extensive professional training in conflict resolution includes work with San Francisco community boards, CDR Associates, the National Association for Mediation in Education, and the Institute for Multi-Track Diplomacy in Washington, D.C.

Koch has presented papers at numerous national and international conferences on conflict resolution, including conferences in Berlin, Sofia, and Bratislava. She studied in the Middle East as a Malone Fellow and is a member of a team of University of Northern Iowa educators working to transform the education system in Slovakia by integrating the ideas and ideals of peacebuilding into the schools. Koch writes and trains extensively in the field of conflict resolution.

THE SPONSORS

National Institute for Dispute Resolution

The National Institute for Dispute Resolution (NIDR) is a nonprofit organization created in 1983 by five leading independent and corporate foundations to promote the development and use of conflict resolution tools and processes. It does this through a variety of means, including publications, technical assistance, education programs, demonstration projects, and limited grants to seed innovation.

While respecting the value of litigation in appropriate circumstances, NIDR strives to expand the availability and improve the use of other conflict resolution processes that have the capacity to provide responsive, timely, and affordable justice. It is guided by the principle that the tensions inherent in conflict situations, if dealt with creatively, can produce positive results. NIDR's key areas of interest include

- *Youth.* Promoting multicultural understanding, prejudice reduction, violence prevention, and the use of cooperative problem-solving tools by young people

- *State and national system reform.* Promoting quality conflict resolution services and programs in state courts, statewide public policy programs, and the use of collaborative problem-solving and dispute resolution tools at the federal and state legislative and policy-making levels

- *Communities.* Promoting the awareness of and access to consensus-building tools that support sustainable communities and promoting the innovative use and deeper understanding of the appropriate and ethical use of consensus-based tools in community settings

Individuals and organizations may join NIDR's Associates program on an annual basis. Associates receive the Institute's newsletter and journal and discounts on other Institute publications. For more information, please write to:

National Institute for Dispute Resolution
1726 M Street, N.W., Suite 500
Washington DC 20036-4502
Phone: (202) 466-4764
Fax: (202) 466-4769

National Association for Mediation in Education

The National Association for Mediation in Education (NAME) was founded in 1984 as a national membership organization to advance conflict resolution programs in schools. It promotes the development, implementation, and institutionalization of school- and university-based conflict resolution programs and curricula. NAME maintains a clearinghouse for information in the field and provides a network of support for conflict resolution programs in education, including a bimonthly newsletter, annual conferences, and regional networking activities. It provides technical assistance and training to existing and developing conflict resolution programs in schools and supports theory and research efforts that increase the understanding of the need for and impact of such programs.

NAME members are pioneers in an exciting new field. They are working to improve the climate in our schools by increasing the conflict resolution skills among all members of the educational community. NAME members have helped to add mediation, negotiation, and group problem-solving skills (such as consensus building) to the traditional disciplinary tools of suspension, detention, and expulsion. By working with school personnel, parents, and students of all ages to build programs in which the school community deals constructively with anger, appreciates diversity, and respects differences, NAME members assist in integrating the principles and practices of constructive conflict resolution into the fabric of school communities around the country.

In 1995, NAME and NIDR decided to form a permanent union between the two organizations, joining together in a mutual effort to improve the climate for learning in our nations' schools and the problem-solving skills of educators and students. NAME, now NIDR's youth program, will remain a member organization; nonmembers can subscribe to NAME's publications and otherwise get information from NAME at NIDR. All inquiries should be made to:

The National Institute for Dispute Resolution
NAME Program Director
1726 M Street, N.W., Suite 500
Washington, D.C. 20036

Conflict Resolution
in the Schools

The Nature of Conflict

Conflict is part of the hidden curriculum in all our educational institutions. It exists in classrooms, lunchrooms, and teachers' lounges, in the principal's office, in the hallways, and on the playgrounds. It exists in college and university faculty meetings, in seminars and labs, and in dorms. It is a primary fact of life—and a constant learning opportunity. Taking charge of what learning occurs from the conflicts that surround us is an important and crucial responsibility of all educators.

This module provides a framework for beginning to examine conflict. It emphasizes three key principles. First, conflict is not inherently positive or negative; rather, it is a natural part of life. Second, conflict affects us all—at all ages, in all settings, within a single culture or community and across all cultures and communities. Third, learning how to look at conflict and how to understand and analyze it can help us shape more effective and productive responses to it.

Objectives

This module enables learners to

- Develop a clear definition of conflict
- Acknowledge the pervasiveness of conflict
- Recognize personal associations with and assumptions about conflict
- Analyze conflicts to enhance understanding
- Explore beliefs about conflict resolution
- Understand factors that affect conflict resolution

Background

There are many definitions of the word *conflict*. Formal definitions range from the more abstract—a "state of disharmony"—to those that signal a more concrete event. Deutsch (1973), for example, states that "conflict exists when incompatible activities occur" (p. 10). Hocker and Wilmot (1991) go further, defining conflict as "an expressed struggle between at least two interdependent parties who perceive incompatible goals, scarce resources and interference from the other party in achieving their goals" (p. 12). In both definitions, words like "activities" and "expressed" point to an action. This is important to note since differences in beliefs, ideas, opinions, and customs may or may not lead to conflict, depending on how, where, and when the differences are behaviorally manifested.

Of all these formal definitions, none denote conflict as either positive or negative. However, for many of us, the connotations of disharmony, incompatibility, and struggle are negative. Our personal associations with the term *conflict* tend to reflect experiences and reveal assumptions about conflict as negative, as something to be avoided, if not eliminated. Personal associations are also often emotional. Conflict means anger, hate, betrayal, and loss.

Moving to an understanding of conflict as organic to the human condition, as a natural phenomenon and a potentially positive occurrence, is critical to improving our responses to conflict. Serious problems often arise not from conflict itself but from our response to it. Thus, understanding conflict is a first step toward productive conflict resolution.

Thinking about definitions and associations may yield a firmer foundation for viewing conflict, but it is only a small, first step toward a positive and productive understanding of conflict. To see conflict clearly, we must be able to see beyond our most familiar and habitual responses. Our feelings, thoughts, physical reactions, and behaviors around conflict stem, at least in part, from the beliefs, assumptions, and experiences with which we were raised. Knowing that conflict is normal and potentially beneficial is not enough to change a lifelong belief that conflict is dangerous or to alter a patterned response of avoidance.

How do we learn to see conflict with insight and perspective and in ways that lead to positive experiences? How do we learn to see conflicts clearly despite the fear and anxiety that often cloud conflict situations? The field of conflict resolution offers a variety of lenses through which to view conflict. These lenses become tools for learning to step out of old beliefs, ideas, and habits and see with new eyes. They can assist in obtaining a wider view, bringing conflict into sharper focus and providing a more distant perspective. Awareness of different ways of viewing a conflict can keep us from becoming locked into a single, unproductive view. There are five ways of looking at conflict that we will explore here. We call them *origins*, *sources*, *types*, *beliefs*, and *stance*. Each has one or two focusing questions to guide our gaze.

Origins

Who are the parties to a given conflict, and how can they be characterized? Conflict can occur within an individual (intrapersonal); between two or more individuals (interpersonal); within a group, organization, institution, or nation (intragroup); or between two or more groups, organizations, institutions, or nations (intergroup). Conflict can occur across these boundaries as well. (For example, a conflict may occur between an individual and an institution.)

Conflict can involve several levels of origin, as well. A conflict at a university involving two faculty members from two departments could be both interpersonal and interdepartmental at once. Conflict can touch, affect, and be expressed at many levels.

Conflict can also occur within a single culture or across two or more cultures. Consider the following definition of culture:

> *Culture* is that part of human interactions and experiences that determine how one feels, acts and thinks. It is through one's culture that one establishes standards to judge right from wrong, beauty and truth, and to make judgments on one's self as well as others. The things and ideas one values and cherishes, how one learns, believes, reacts, etc. are all immersed in and impacted by one's culture. It is one's culture that prescribes the very sense of the individual's scope of reality [Nakagawa, 1986, p. 6].

Culture is a term that has undergone substantial change in recent decades. Classic notions of culture grew out of the study of well-bounded, homogeneous societies. In our complex, global world we tend to use the term more broadly, to refer to a set of behaviors or generalized social characteristics associated with groups defined by a wide range of characteristics. Race, ethnicity, and religion are seen as defining cultural groups, but so are gender, marital status, sexual orientation, occupation, profession, age, geographical region, and socioeconomic status. This definition of culture suggests that each person belongs to and is influenced by many cultures. Which cultural group is primary for an individual may change within a given day as he or she moves through different settings and activities and over a lifetime as his or her underlying needs and interests shift.

Viewing culture in this dynamic way, we can see that the cultural characteristics of those involved in a conflict are an important element. The degree to which cultural elements are similar or different will have an impact on the conflict. Perceptions, expectations, behaviors, and communication patterns are all rooted in culture.

It is not a question of whether or not cultural factors are involved in a conflict, however, but of how cultural differences affect it. By identifying the cultural characteristics of all the parties involved, we are better able to view cultural differences *as* differences rather than as deficiencies, with fewer distortions of prejudice and stereotyping. Understanding each other's cultural codes (language, art, traditions, and behaviors) is an essential step in both conflict prevention and conflict resolution.

If we identify the origin of a conflict as interpersonal, for example, we would step further back from the details of the people or organization. This enables us to apply what we know about interpersonal communication and organizational dynamics, generally, to our understanding of the conflict. It also allows us to step back far enough to see all the levels of the conflict—whether, for example, a conflict is really interpersonal or actually includes other dimensions. This enables us, again, to bring a fuller set of relevant knowledge and experience to understanding the immediate details.

We accomplish another increase in perspective and understanding when we identify the cultural characteristics of the parties involved. With greater perspective and understanding we can begin to see the complexity, issues, time frames, and other factors that influence how conflict is expressed, how it develops, and how it can be resolved.

Sources

What is this conflict about? How can it be broadly characterized? While the term *origins* refers to who is involved, *sources* refers to what the conflict is about. Conflict exists when actions come into opposition. The content of that opposition—that is, the source of the conflict—is another view into a conflict. The purpose of this lens is not to capture the details of each party's story but to see the broad category within which the conflict fits. It is easy to become lost in the details of what a conflict is about. To see more clearly, we need to step back, note the general characteristics of the conflict, and bring forward our general knowledge concerning that category of problem.

For example, resources are the focus of much conflict. Within this category, we could identify subcategories such as scarcity, control, access, possessions, territory, space, and time. A colleague might say, "I am furious that Harold moved into the second-floor office," but it could be more helpful—and just as true—if they said,

"I am having a conflict with Harold over scarce space resources." The latter opens the question of origins. Is this really an interpersonal conflict? It causes those involved to consider what they know about space resources, space allocations, and so on.

Many writers in the conflict resolution field offer frameworks for further categorizing conflicts. Christopher Moore (1986) suggests that conflicts fall into these categories: conflicts over relationships, values, data, interests, or structures. A psychological framework is seen as helpful by some. Schrumpf, Crawford, and Usadel (1991) rely on Glasser's control theory to categorize all conflicts in relation to four psychological needs: the need to belong, the need for power, the need for freedom, and the need for fun (Schrumpf, Crawford, & Usadel, 1991; Glasser, 1984).

Drawing from organizational theory, Wall (1985) puts all sources of conflict into three major groups: conflicts arising from interdependence, conflicts arising from differences in goals, and conflicts arising from differences in perception. Tichy (1983), also using an organizational-change model, suggests these three main focuses for conflict: technical (conflict over designs), political (conflict over rewards and punishments), and cultural (conflict over expected norms and values). Technical issues include the way individuals, groups, and organizations assemble resources, people, and technology to produce outputs. Political issues (familiar to anyone who works in an organization) include who gets what rewards or punishments and for which activities. Cultural issues, as Tichy defines them, are similar to those we have already discussed.

There is no single "right" categorization framework. There are benefits in all of them. Each can be instrumental in providing a broader perspective and in calling forth a richer array of knowledge and responses. Insight into complexity, possible intervention points, strategies, and resolutions can emerge from categorizing a conflict.

Types

What type of conflict is this in terms of where movement toward resolution is most likely to occur? What type of conflict is this in terms of potential ease of resolution? Specific sources of conflict and general categories of conflicts can be analyzed in terms of their focus and their likelihood of moving toward a resolution.

Moore (1986) suggests that there are two basic types of conflict: unnecessary and genuine. Unnecessary conflicts have communication and perception problems at their root, while genuine conflicts arise from more concrete differences. Under Moore's typology, relationship, value, and data conflicts are more often unnecessary and may simply disappear with appropriate and clear communication, while interest and structural conflicts are genuine and will require a different level of effort to resolve.

Deutsch (1973) offers a more detailed typology, encompassing six categories. Each points to different paths for resolution. Each offers questions that are useful for analyzing a conflict:

1. *Veridical:* Does the conflict exist objectively? Is it unlikely to be easily resolved?
2. *Contingent:* Is the conflict dependent on circumstances that can be easily changed?
3. *Displaced:* Is the expressed conflict different from the central conflict?
4. *Misattributed:* Is the conflict expressed between the wrong parties?
5. *Latent:* Is the conflict submerged, not yet occurring?
6. *False:* Is the conflict based on misunderstanding or misperception?

Applying Tichy's perspective on organizational change (1983) to a conflict scenario, each source of conflict can be seen as fitting within a general arena of organizational activity. Thus, technical conflicts find movement through technical design, conflicts over political allocations find movement in organizational rewards, and cultural conflicts require examination of expected norms and values.

Questions and typologies such as these offer a further set of resources for understanding a conflict. They help us get to a sense of where movement might occur—by changing an external circumstance, by engaging other parties or issues, by clarifying previous communications, or by examining norms and values.

Beliefs

What do the parties believe about the goals and outcomes of conflict resolution? That is, what do they believe can happen? The range of resolution scenarios accepted, understood, or valued by participants is an important factor in understanding how a conflict is expressed and develops. Scenarios range from a competitive, win-lose perspective to pure cooperation, where either all parties win or all lose. How we view possibilities for resolving conflicts often depends upon our beliefs and attitudes about relationships, the strength of our goal focus, our personal characteristics, and our comfort with assertiveness and aggressiveness. Some people only know anger, aggression, and winning or losing. Some people only know fear and avoidance. Some people have a variety of responses that they use in different circumstances and with a range of outcomes. If disputants expect only a win-lose outcome, that will affect and likely determine what happens. Knowing what each person involved in a conflict believes about how conflicts can end suggests points and strategies for intervention.

Culture is likely to be an important variable, affecting disputants' view of conflict and their general goals for resolution. Some understanding of how different cultures view conflict can be helpful in approaching the question of what beliefs about conflict will influence how it is resolved. Cultural conceptions concerning honor, shame, loyalty, privacy, authority, and obedience, among others, can have a major impact on what will constitute a satisfying outcome for each party. What constitutes resolution in one culture is not necessarily resolution in another. Thus both the culture of the parties involved and the culture of the setting in which the conflict occurs will influence the outcome.

Schools, organizations, and groups all develop cultures of their own. Each develops and communicates to its members a view of conflict. When an organization or group is a party to a conflict, the culture of that organization or group is an important factor in determining how it will respond. Organizational or group culture is an important factor even when the conflict is truly personal and between two people but is expressed within the group or organization. In the school culture, for example, resolution of conflict is typically understood as obedience to a higher authority. That view of conflict resolution may not be congruent with a member of the school community's primary culture, peer culture, or family culture. When that person is involved in a conflict with the school or a conflict that occurs on school grounds, the culture of the school and the school's view of how conflicts are resolved become important factors. Educators need to be especially mindful of the fact that youth has a culture of its own. Defined not only by age but also by behaviors, clothing, hairstyles, language, and music, youth cultures bring their own attitudes and beliefs to conflicts.

There are a variety of models for expanding our vision of what can result from conflict. In *The Genius of Sitting Bull*, Murphy (1993) describes what he calls heroic leadership. The qualities of heroic leadership are commitment, integrity, empowerment, healing, statesmanship, strategic vision, courage, guardianship, and success. Heroic leadership is a preventive approach to conflict, as opposed to dominance and crisis management, which are reactive in nature. Leadership models, peacemaking models, religious models, different cultural models, and mediation and consensus decision making can all inspire new beliefs and views of how conflicts can end. All contribute to positive outcomes in conflict situations. For the purposes of beginning to understand and analyze a conflict, we are concerned here with simply posing the question of what beliefs about conflict resolution are currently guiding the parties involved.

Stance

What will satisfy the parties in the conflict? How can we characterize what they say they want? The final area to examine in preparing to resolve conflict is the disputants' stance. We will look at three factors that contribute to their overall stance: their *positions, interests,* and *needs.* Each of these areas can shape a disputant's stance in a conflict. Understanding whether disputants are speaking from position, needs, or interests is helpful in finding ways into and through a conflict. Information on stance is another part of the conflict map.

• *Positions* represent the most common initial stance taken by parties in a conflict. Positions simply define what the parties think they want. The problem with a positional stance is that positions can be challenged and opposed. Positions tend to focus on specific, concrete outcomes, and thus they limit the notion of resolution to the achievement of those specific goals. Positions do not leave much room for exploring and problem solving: you get what you want, you compromise what you want, or you don't get what you want. It is very important, in analyzing a conflict, to determine whether disputants are taking positional stances.

• *Interests* represent the context in which a position may exist. Interests are less subject to debate. Interests may converge. Two sisters fight over possession of the mixing bowl after their mother has poured the chocolate cake mix into the pan. Each begins with the positional stance of wanting to be first to get her share of the sticky remains. Each has powerful arguments. "I'm older." "I help more." "You took more last time." Determining who should be first to gain possession or debating the arguments does little to resolve the conflict. Moving beyond positions, however, opens the way to the discovery of common interests that can be fully met. In this instance, perhaps their interests are not in conflict, since one wants to lick the spoon and the other wants to skim the batter from the bowl with her fingers.

• *Needs* represent the even broader context within which interests exist. Unmet physical and psychological needs underlie many, if not all, conflicts. Even if such needs are not expressed, the satisfaction of them may be essential to a full resolution of the conflict. There are many frameworks for analyzing and understanding basic human needs. Previously we cited the four needs derived from Glasser's control theory (1984): needs for belonging, power, freedom, and fun. Maslow's hierarchy of needs (1968), ranging from the physical to the transcendent, is another framework familiar to many. Diamond (1994) identifies the psychological needs of groups as identity, security, vitality, and community, noting that most prejudice, misunderstanding, and conflict within and among groups stem from these four basic group needs. Again, there is no single psychological schematic that is universally accepted as full and complete across cultures, theories, beliefs, and experiences. The point is simply to pose the question, What needs underlie the expressed conflict, the identified position? Using a framework of psychological needs—individual or group—simply assists in how and where to look for needs.

Psychological needs exist within cultural contexts, as do interests and positions. Looking at the cultural expectations and norms influencing each party can be valuable in reaching a full understanding of that party's positions, interests, and needs. Looking at differences in those cultural norms and expectations (individual, group, organizational) is also essential in interpreting expressed positions, interests, or needs.

The ability to analyze conflict plays a part in moving toward more productive experiences with conflict. Understanding the role and nature of needs, interests, and positions is an important component of that analysis. A satisfying resolution to a given conflict is more likely to occur when

- Those involved understand the underlying needs that must be addressed.
- The focus is on exploring everyone's interests.
- Positions are distinguished from interests.
- Interests are defined rather than assumed.
- Interests rather than positions are the focus for discussion and responses.
- Conflicting interests are seen as a shared problem, to be solved mutually.
- Cultural differences are recognized and understood.

In addition to learning ways of looking at conflict (such as examining origins, sources, and stances), we must accept the notion that conflict is everywhere. It exists at all ages, in all settings, in all cultures. Research on conflict with children as young as age two shows patterns of conflict similar to what adults experience. People's conflicts become more complex as they mature.

Over time, we squabble less over toys and more over influence and control of each other. In general, however, childhood conflicts follow the same general pattern as adult conflicts: they originate, they have events and reactions, and they finally resolve.

Children have needs, interests, and positions, just like adults. As they mature, they move from only being able to act on or state their position to being able to identify their interests. Primary developmental tasks of young children include learning problem-solving skills and social cooperation. Children need help learning how to recognize, respond to, and solve the variety of conflicts and problems they encounter. Thus conflict resolution skills fit within developmentally appropriate curricula for toddlers and preschoolers as well as for elementary and secondary school students.

Just as we must gain new conflict resolution skills to meet our changing developmental needs, so too must we develop new conflict resolution strategies to fit an increasingly multicultural society. We must face the differences between cultures without fear and with respect. At the same time, we must recognize that there are no simple answers, no "right" and "wrong," when cultural norms and values clash. In the absence of generalized answers, conflict resolution offers processes for reflection and dialogue that are essential to cross-cultural understanding and dialogue.

Conflict surrounds us. It offers rich opportunities for learning about our culture, values, needs, and interests as well as the culture, values, needs, and interests of others. Unfortunately, most of us view conflict with trepidation, if not fear. The field of conflict resolution offers a variety of tools for stepping back from a conflict and examining it more objectively. What is the source and type of the conflict? What are the characteristics of the parties involved? What are their beliefs and stances? These questions enable us to awaken our curiosity and to see a conflict more fully, whether we are directly involved or merely observing. They help us bring to our observations a broader set of knowledge and experience.

References

Deutsch, M. (1973). *The resolution of conflict: Constructive and restrictive processes.* New Haven, CT: Yale University Press.

Diamond, L. (1994). *Beyond win/win: The heroic journey of conflict transformation.* (Occasional Paper No. 4). Washington, DC: Institute for Multi-Track Diplomacy.

Glasser, W. (1984). *Control theory.* New York: HarperCollins.

Hocker, J., & Wilmot, W. (1991). *Interpersonal conflict* (3rd ed.). Dubuque, IA: W. C. Brown.

Maslow, A. (1968). *Toward a psychology of being.* (2nd ed.) New York: Van Nostrand Reinhold.

Moore, C. (1986). *The mediation process: Practical strategies for resolving conflict.* San Francisco: Jossey-Bass.

Murphy, E. C., & Snell, M. (1993). *The genius of Sitting Bull: 13 heroic strategies for today's business leaders.* Englewood Cliffs, NJ: Prentice-Hall.

Nakagawa, M. (1986). "A closer look at culture." *Your Public Schools,* 25(11), 6.

Schrumpf, F., Crawford, D., & Usadel, H. (1991). *Peer mediation: Conflict resolution in schools.* Champaign, IL: Research Press.

Tichy, N. M. (1983). *Managing strategic change: Technical, political, and cultural dynamics.* New York: Wiley.

Wall, J. A. (1985). *Negotiation: Theory and practice.* Glenview, IL: Scott, Foresman.

Exercises

Learning about conflict and developing conflict resolution skills are active endeavors. The following exercises provide ways of furthering an understanding of the issues discussed in this chapter.

Exercise 1.1. Definitions of Conflict

NOTE: Besides presenting various definitions, this exercise can help the members of a class group begin getting acquainted with one another. If you use it for this additional purpose, allow a few more minutes at each stage of the exercise where class members work together.

Objectives

- Develop a clear definition of conflict
- Acknowledge the pervasiveness of conflict
- Recognize personal associations with and assumptions about conflict

Procedures

1. Ask each participant to write a definition for *conflict* on a piece of paper. Allow three to five minutes for this step.

2. Have everyone pair up. Have each pair compare their definitions and then draft a joint definition. Allow eight to ten minutes for this step.

3. Direct pairs to join into groups of four, again compare definitions, and then jointly draft a single definition for the foursome. Allow fifteen to twenty minutes for this step.

4. Have the groups share their definitions with the entire group. Discuss differences in definitions, common elements, and changes from individual definitions to group definition. *Note:* Make sure that the discussion following the exercise points out that conflict is, by definition, neither positive nor negative.

 ## Exercise 1.2. Conflict Metaphors

NOTE: Metaphors can illuminate aspects of a conflict that might otherwise remain hidden. This exercise helps participants understand conflict more clearly and identify common images of conflict.

Objectives

- Develop a clear definition of conflict
- Acknowledge the pervasiveness of conflict
- Recognize personal associations with and assumptions about conflict

Procedures

1. Ask participants to think of metaphors describing conflict and give you a silent signal—a clenched fist, perhaps—when they have come up with something. If participants find it difficult to think of metaphors, give some examples to start the process: conflict is a battle, conflict is an onion, conflict is an airplane out of control. Allow two to three minutes for this step.

2. Ask participants to gather in groups of four to describe and explain their metaphors to one another. Allow five minutes for this step.

3. Ask the groups to discuss ways to manage conflict in keeping with their metaphors. (For example, if conflict is like a battle, waving a flag of truce might be a step in managing it.) Allow five minutes for this step.

4. Next, ask the groups to translate their metaphorical solutions into practical solutions. (For example, a flag of truce might translate into a message to the other side indicating readiness to talk about the conflict.) Allow five minutes for this step.

5. Reassemble the class and ask someone from each group to share one of the metaphors and explanations the group came up with. Lead a discussion of the resulting ideas, pointing out common elements and differences.

6. Summarize the discussion and then share several formal definitions of conflict. (The first paragraph of the Background section gives some examples.)

Exercise 1.3. Words That Mean Conflict

NOTE: This exercise can be done either as described here or in the individual, small-group, and whole-group steps outlined in the first two exercises.

Objectives

- Develop a clear definition of conflict
- Acknowledge the pervasiveness of conflict
- Recognize personal associations with and assumptions about conflict

Procedures

1. Ask participants to think back on the last week and remember any conflicts they witnessed, participated in, or heard about. Repeat this instruction to cover the last month and the last year.

2. Ask participants what words come to mind when they think about conflict. Allow participants to jot some down and then share them with the class. Write the words where everyone can see them, so as to build a complete list for the group. If the exercise doesn't evoke general participation, try some additional prompts, such as "What feelings do you associate with conflict? What words mean conflict?"

3. Guide a group discussion about the impact our associations with conflict have on how we approach and respond to it. Share some basic definitions, and emphasize the natural existence of conflict, its neutrality, and its potential for benefits and learning.

 ## Exercise 1.4. Ways of Analyzing Conflict

NOTE: Before resolution can occur, participants in a conflict need to understand completely what the conflict is about. Analyzing conflict carefully is necessary to explore the issues that have caused the problem.

Objectives

- Acknowledge the pervasiveness of conflict
- Analyze conflicts to enhance understanding
- Explore beliefs about conflict resolution
- Understand factors that affect resolution

Procedures

1. Introduce the concept of analyzing or mapping conflict, stressing the need for perspective, understanding, and insight. Introduce the "lenses" that can help one see into and through a conflict: origins, sources, types, beliefs, and stances. Hand out copies of the list of focusing questions (Exhibit 1.1).

2. Present information on the origins of conflict, including the notion of culture. Point out that you can understand a conflict only when you understand the backgrounds of the participants. Thus it is always necessary to ask the origins question: *Who are the parties to the conflict, and how can they be characterized?*

3. Have participants present lists of possible sources of conflict and different ways of categorizing these sources. You can offer Moore's grouping of conflicts (1986) as an example if the class seems to find the concept difficult. Explain how categorizing conflicts can assist them by providing perspective and helping them draw on more of their experience. Use the following incident to illustrate the shift in focus from telling the story of a conflict to identifying the kind of conflict involved.

> Students of Mrs. Jones, a math teacher at the John Jay Middle School, have brought her their typing practice assignment. Their typing sentence, assigned by Mr. Henry, was "Mrs. Jones is too old and too fat to swim five hundred laps at the MS fund-raiser." The whole school knows about this incident. Mrs. Jones is furious. Mr. Henry thinks it's funny and that Mrs. Jones needs to get off her high horse. Mrs. Jones was recently voted most popular teacher by the students; Mr. Henry, on the other hand, was awarded a dead rat by one student (it appeared anonymously on his desk). He is not beloved by students.

What is this conflict about? On the surface one could say this conflict seems based on jealousy. Yet, does naming it in this way help us understand a path to its resolution? What if we looked at it from the standpoint of the psychological need to belong? Are there value conflicts embedded that result in Mrs. Jones being popular and Mr. Henry unpopular with students? Does it take us to a deeper level of understanding to explore the conflict as arising over the political allocation of rewards (Tichy, 1983)? Is the school culture supporting Mr. Henry's development as a teacher? Is it contributing to a negative relationship between the two teachers?

Make sure the group sees how changing the focus changes what we know and seek to learn about a conflict. Point out that it is always useful to trace the sources of a conflict by asking, *What is this conflict about? How can it be broadly characterized?*

4. Present information on types of conflicts. Note that this is just a further categorization, aimed at providing insight into possible paths for movement toward resolution. Explain Moore's (1986) and Deutsch's (1973) typologies. Discuss the questions to be answered related to types: *What type of conflict is this in terms of where movement toward resolution is most likely to occur? What type of conflict is this in terms of potential ease of resolution?*

5. Have participants come up with a list of the general outcomes possible in a conflict. Make sure the final list includes the entire set of outcomes (win-win, win-lose, compromise, lose-lose, and so on). Discuss how visions of the possibilities for resolution affect a conflict. Introduce the notion of cultural difference with respect to what is understood or accepted as a resolution. Discuss this question related to beliefs: *What do the parties believe about the goals and outcomes of conflict resolution? That is, what do they believe can happen?*

6. Present information on the different stances disputants may take. Look at positions, interests, and needs and the value of clarifying interests and needs. Provide (or elicit from the group) examples of different types of conflict: conflicts in which positions are opposed but interests converge; conflicts in which positions and interests are opposed but goals converge; conflicts in which positions, interests, and goals are opposed but values converge. Discuss the necessity of going beyond positions to reach a satisfactory resolution.

Exhibit 1.1.   Key Questions for Analyzing Conflict

- *Origins.* Who are the parties to the conflict? How can they be characterized?
- *Sources.* What is this conflict about? How can it be broadly characterized?
- *Types.* What type of conflict is this in terms of where movement toward resolution is most likely to occur? What type of conflict is this in terms of potential ease of resolution?
- *Beliefs.* What do the parties believe about the goals and outcomes of conflict resolution? That is, what do they believe can happen?
- *Stance.* What are the parties in the conflict seeking to satisfy? How can we characterize what they say they want?

Exercise 1.5. The Beautiful Butterfly Case

NOTE: Use this exercise to introduce the concepts of positions, interests, and needs. Use it after discussing the influence of beliefs on conflict resolution but before addressing the factors affecting resolution.

Alternatively, use the exercise to teach the skill of separating positions from interests and needs, which relies on asking open-ended and clarifying questions. For this purpose, omit the exercise here but bring it in later. In Exercise 3.1 you will find procedures based on this hypothetical situation that are especially tailored to teaching these skills.

Objectives

- Acknowledge the pervasiveness of conflict
- Analyze conflicts to enhance understanding
- Explore beliefs about conflict resolution
- Understand factors that affect resolution

Procedures

1. Have the participants pair off, and give each partner Exhibit 1.2a, "Role for Dr. T. P. James," or Exhibit 1.2b, "Role for Dr. P. B. Hirera."

2. Direct each pair to settle the conflict. Tell them that both their jobs are riding on working this deal out in their own company's favor. Allow ten to fifteen minutes for them to read the role and negotiate.

3. Reassemble the class and ask each pair how they solved the situation. Usually, at least one pair will have figured out that Dr. James needs the cocoons (the casing around the larval stage of the butterfly), and that Dr. Hirera needs the mature butterflies. Thus, each can have what he wants. Explore how they came to this discovery.

Exhibit 1.2a.   The Beautiful Butterfly Case: Role for Dr. T. P. James

Dr. R. L. Lymanski, founder and director of the Lepidopterist Sanctuary of the Americas, recently passed away. Since the sanctuary cannot afford to continue his work, the sanctuary's land, its butterfly collections, and its rare living butterflies are being sold at an IRS auction.

You are Dr. T. P. James, a research chemist with a small pharmaceutical firm. You have been developing a topical cream to prevent skin cancer. Many years ago, you thought that you were on a solid track to solving this growing problem. Today the need is even more urgent, as people are panicked about the alarming growth of skin cancer, even among young children.

Unfortunately, the Impricate butterfly, whose cocoon might have contained an essential element for the development of the topical cream, became extinct before you could identify and duplicate the precise chemical compound. All your investors but one have pulled out. If you can't demonstrate that you have a viable formula, you will lose everything. You need exactly twenty-five Impricates to complete your analysis and perfect the formula. You now have it on good authority that the Lepidopterist Sanctuary has twenty-five Impricate butterfly cocoons that will go on auction tomorrow. Based on your prior research results, your remaining investor has put up $5,000 for the Impricate butterflies.

You were feeling quite confident that you would have no problem obtaining the butterflies, but a colleague has heard that a Dr. P. B. Hirera has traveled from Brazil to claim the butterflies on behalf of the Brazilian government. You have decided to meet with this Dr. Hirera to make sure you will have access to the butterflies and will not be outbid. Your future and the health of hundreds of thousands of people depend on your success.

Exhibit 1.2b.   The Beautiful Butterfly Case: Role for Dr. P. B. Hirera

Dr. R. L. Lymanski, founder and director of the Lepidopterist Sanctuary of the Americas, recently passed away. Since the sanctuary cannot afford to continue his work, the sanctuary's land, its butterfly collections, and its living, nonlocal butterflies are being sold at an IRS auction. Among the items being sold are twenty-five Impricate butterfly cocoons.

You are Dr. P. B. Hirera, minister of environmental policies for Brazil. Preserving the rain forest, both as an ecosystem and as a functioning economic and social community for its indigenous Indian people, has been your lifelong goal. One of the key problems you currently face is the loss of the Magoriji tree, an essential part of the forest's ecology and a basic source of food for the native people. The extinction of the Impricate butterfly, the only insect that pollinates the Magoriji tree, was a severe blow. Experiments with hand-pollination have not worked. Other experiments have also failed. Twenty-five cocoons, from which twenty-five adult Impricate butterflies will emerge, will be just enough to start the needed pollination; any fewer and it would still be hopeless. Your government is seeking direct access to the butterflies. Should that fail, you have been authorized to spend up to $15,000 for the butterflies.

You understand that a commercial enterprise wants the twenty-five cocoons for research purposes and that a Dr. James has made an appointment to talk with you. Dr. James can talk all he wants, but the butterflies belong to Brazil and in your beloved rain forest. They are the forest's—and its people's—only hope.

 ## Exercise 1.6. Conflict Analysis

NOTE: This exercise needs to follow information and discussion on ways to analyze conflict.

Objectives

- Acknowledge the pervasiveness of conflict
- Analyze conflicts to enhance understanding
- Explore beliefs about conflict resolution
- Understand factors that affect resolution

Procedures

1. Ask each person to think about a complex conflict, either resolved or ongoing, in which he or she was or is involved. Ask participants to map their conflicts using the questions related to origins, sources, types, beliefs, and stances. Allow fifteen to twenty minutes for this. Give each Exhibit 1.3, "Seeing Conflict Clearly."

2. Have the class as a group discuss their assessments and questions. Explore which lenses seemed most productive. Which were most accessible? Which were more difficult to uncover?

Exhibit 1.3.   Seeing Conflict Clearly: A Discussion Guide

How can we look at conflict so as to gain perspective, understanding, insight, and clarity?

1. Look at the origins.
   a. Who are the parties to this conflict? How can they be characterized?
   b. Who is the conflict between?
      Two individuals (interpersonal)
      Within a person (intrapersonal)
      Two groups (intergroup)
      Within a group (intragroup)
   c. What are the cultures of the parties involved?
      Race
      Gender
      Socioeconomic status
      Ethnicity
      Religion
      Sexual orientation
      Occupation
      Age
      Region
2. Look at the sources.
   a. What is this conflict about? How can it be generally described?
   b. What are some basic sources of conflict? (Resources are one example. Develop as complete a list as you can here.)
   c. Can any of these be broken down into subcategories? (For example, resources can be considered in terms of scarcity, control, access, possessions, and territory. Develop similar lists for each source of conflict you have identified.)
   d. How can these be grouped to increase understanding? (For example, Moore sees categories in terms of relationship conflicts, value conflicts, data conflicts, interest conflicts, and structure conflicts. Wall sees interdependence conflicts, differences in goals, and differences in perceptions. List other possible groupings.)
   e. How does our understanding and our perspective change when we talk about conflict in terms of categories instead of in terms of the details of the story?
3. Look at the type of conflict. (This section analyzes the key question of conflict type in terms of identifying where movement toward resolution is most likely to occur and in terms of potential ease of resolution.)
   a. Is the conflict based solely or largely on a misperception or misunderstanding? (If yes, this may be what Moore calls an unnecessary conflict and Deutsch calls a false one. Such conflicts are often easily resolved by improving communication.)
   b. Does the conflict exist objectively, in fixed conditions? (If yes, this may be what Deutsch calls veridical and Moore calls necessary conflict. Such conflicts tend to continue despite improved communications, as resolution requires some change in external conditions.)
   c. Is the conflict dependent on conditions that can be easily changed? (If yes, the conflict may be necessary but easily remedied through

changing external circumstances. Deutsch calls this a contingent conflict.)

    d. Is the expressed conflict really the central conflict? (If not, resolution is unlikely. One needs to know what the real conflict is about in order to see where movement might occur. Deutsch calls these displaced conflicts.)

    e. Is the conflict being expressed between the right parties? (If not, as with displaced conflicts, resolution is difficult. Finding where movement toward resolution can happen will most likely depend on having the right people involved. Deutsch calls these misattributed conflicts.)

    f. Is the real conflict submerged, not yet occurring? (A small conflict may signal the beginning of a change in awareness or values that may lead to a much larger conflict later. A conflict over household chores, for example, might really be about household chores, or it might be a displaced conflict sparked by distress over a forgotten anniversary—or it might be the beginning of a much larger change of consciousness about gender roles. Deutsch calls the third type a latent conflict.)

4. Look at beliefs about resolution.

    a. What do the parties believe can happen?
       Everybody wins or everybody loses.
       One side wins and one side loses.
       Everybody must compromise.

    b. What affects how we view the potential resolutions of conflicts?
       Beliefs and attitudes about relationships
       Strength of our focus on goals
       Personal characteristics
       Past experience
       Comfort with assertiveness and aggression
       Cultural norms, values, and expectations
       Culture of the setting in which conflict occurs

5. Look at the stance.

    a. What are the parties in the conflict trying to satisfy? How can we characterize what they say they want?
       Are the parties taking positions? (Focus on a specific concrete outcome.)
       Are the parties identifying their interests? (Focus on the broader goals that each side is trying to achieve. Bear in mind that opening positions represent only one interpretation of how the goal could be met.)
       Are the parties acknowledging their needs? (Focus on the underlying drive that needs to be met, remembering that interests sit within the context of needs.)
       Are the parties aware of the cultural factors influencing their expression of positions, interests, or needs? (Focus on cultural norms and expectations in order to understand differences.)

    b. What contributes to achieving a satisfying resolution?
       The people involved understand that underlying needs must be addressed.
       Everyone's interests are explored.
       Positions are distinguished from interests.

Interests are defined, not assumed.
Interests, rather than positions, are the focus for discussion.
Conflicting interests are seen as a shared problem to be solved.
Cultural differences are recognized and understood.

 ## Exercise 1.7. Conflict Sculpture

NOTE: In this exercise, participants form a living sculpture that illustrates various aspects of a conflict. This exercise can be used at the end of the module as an example of another technique for seeing into conflict. Alternatively, it can be used at the beginning, ahead of the other presentations and discussions, to introduce the idea of analyzing conflict. If planned as an introductory activity, a mixer or icebreaker should probably precede it.

Objectives

- Acknowledge the pervasiveness of conflict
- Analyze conflicts to enhance understanding
- Explore beliefs about conflict resolution
- Understand factors that affect resolution

Procedures

1. Describe the conflict sculpture exercise.

2. Ask for a volunteer to describe a conflict. Ask for other volunteers to participate in forming a living sculpture to illustrate that conflict. Then have the first volunteer arrange the others into positions forming a tableau (still portrait) that physically symbolizes the individuals, postures, relationships, and emotions in that conflict. Advise the director to feel free to assign roles, move participants around, and pose them to illustrate emotions and actions. For example, a scene might show two students (caught fighting) and their two parents in the principal's office. The two students might be placed squaring off with fists raised. One parent is behind his or her child with fists raised. The other parent is turned away from his or her child and is shaking hands with the principal.

3. Thank the director, and tell the participants in the scene to move slowly in the direction they each think their character would naturally move. Ask participants to remain silent and to use only movement and gestures to express emotions and actions. For example, the above scene in motion might lead to the one parent grabbing his or her child and yanking him away, while the second parent moves closer to the principal, ignoring his or her own child, who tries to become invisible.

4. Stop the action as soon as patterns are evident. Discuss possible intervention points, outcomes, and consequences with the actors in the scene first and then with those observing.

The Concepts and Skills of Conflict Resolution

The theoretical and applied aspects of conflict resolution build on foundational values, beliefs, attitudes, and skills. In the same way that a building cannot remain standing without firm support, commitment and quality in teaching conflict resolution is not possible without an orientation toward tolerance, cooperation, and collaboration as well as communication and thinking skills that enable rather than disable conflict resolution processes.

This module presents the values, beliefs, attitudes, and skills that are essential prerequisites to successful conflict resolution. It is designed to help conflict resolution educators examine, elucidate, and enhance foundational orientations and skills within the context of their own and their students' professional practice.

Objectives

This module enables learners to

- Identify values, beliefs, and attitudes associated with conflict resolution
- Examine their own orientation toward conflict resolution, identifying attitudes and beliefs that may enhance or detract from their effectiveness as a conflict resolution practitioner
- Identify and enhance communication skills that improve conflict resolution processes
- Identify and enhance thinking skills that improve conflict resolution processes

- Examine and apply the foundational orientations and skills of conflict resolution in the context of the education environment

Background

There is an old teaching story about a holy man who retreats into a mountain cave to meditate and seek enlightenment. At the end of ten years, he returns to his village to share his peace and wisdom. He speaks to the gathering crowd slowly and gently: "My dearest brothers and sisters, for ten years I have been—"

"Tell us what you learned!" shouts an impatient young man. Clearing his throat, the holy man begins again, "My dearest brothers and sisters, for ten years—"

"What did you learn that will help us?" yells the young man. "I'm coming to that," the holy man replies, a touch testily. After two more increasingly agitated starts and two more interruptions, the holy man finally shares his most important achievement. Red-faced and shaking his fist at the impatient youth, he screams, "I learned to conquer anger!"

It's a good story for teaching about human nature and conflict. As the story shows, the real test of our skills in handling conflict comes when we interact with others. Often our actions are less noble than our words or our idea of how we are or think we ought to be. We begin to go off track not only when the gap between our goals and our behavior widens but also when we become attached to unrealistic goals. Goals for a conflict-free, anger-free, stress-free existence, for example, are likely to remain frustratingly unmet.

Self-Assessment

Assessing and reflecting on one's own behaviors can help narrow the gap between words and deeds and keep goals realistic. But examining one's behaviors related to conflict can be intimidating. First, conflict is often associated with many negative feelings and painful experiences. Second, looking at behavior is usually associated with finding fault and judging. These are two good reasons to avoid self-assessment.

Willingness to examine one's conflict behaviors can be strengthened by focusing on three core beliefs. The first of these is the belief that conflict comes naturally and organically with social interaction. Everyone experiences conflict. Once this belief is accepted, the idea that one is "bad" for being involved in conflicts loses force, and it becomes easier to delve into one's conflict experiences. While there is evidence that human beings can solve problems (and we often wish there were more evidence), there is no evidence that human beings can live together without conflict arising.

The second belief is that one can choose the conflict behaviors and approach one uses in each event. Of course, the more one knows about one's behaviors, the more control and choice one has about those behaviors. Given the choice in a card game, most people would prefer to play with as many cards as are allowed—and without a blindfold. With respect to our own actions, we often choose to use only a few behaviors while refusing to look at the others in our repertoire. We have to look at ourselves in order to be able to choose those behaviors that will be most effective in a given situation and contain those that we have seen to be ineffective.

The third belief is that conflict can be productive and beneficial. Problems get solved when conflicts are successfully resolved. Communication improves as conflicts move toward resolution and in the aftermath of effective conflict resolution processes. Cultural differences may be better understood following a conflict. But we have to be active, self-aware, and reflective participants in conflict in order for it to be productive.

Tools to assist in the process of examining conflict behaviors are plentiful and varied. Most explore two or more dimensions of conflict behavior and suggest different profiles of conflict response. While several such instruments are described in this module, it is important to remember that any assessment can only measure perceptions of behavior and cannot take into account the differences in approach that are likely to occur under changing circumstances. Self-assessment is valuable not for the label it produces but for the information it provides, information that can become a catalyst for self-reflection and a stimulus for learning more about conflict. The following approaches to measuring and categorizing conflict behaviors are provided to suggest different ways of looking at these behaviors.

The Thomas-Kilmann Conflict Mode Instrument (Kilmann & Thomas, 1975, pp. 971–980) analyzes conflict behaviors using assertiveness and cooperativeness dimensions. Assertiveness is defined as the extent to which individuals attempt to satisfy their own concerns, while cooperativeness is defined as the extent to which individuals attempt to satisfy others' concerns. Within these two behavioral dimensions the authors define five methods of dealing with conflict: competing, collaborating, compromising, avoiding, and accommodating. Competing is assertive and uncooperative, accommodating is unassertive and cooperative, avoiding is unassertive and uncooperative, collaborating is both assertive and cooperative, and compromising is at the midpoint of both the assertive and cooperative dimensions.

Thomas and Kilmann suggest that there are appropriate uses for all five methods. For example,

- Competing can be helpful in an emergency.
- Collaborating is important when both sets of concerns are too important to be compromised.
- Compromising can be appropriate when goals are only moderately important.
- Avoiding may be appropriate when an issue is trivial or when other issues are more pressing.
- Accommodating may be highly appropriate when one is wrong.

Hocker and Wilmot (1991) developed a Conflict Attitudes Assessment, not as a specific measure of conflict style but as a tool for encouraging introspection and generating discussion. Their Conflict Attitudes Assessment assists users in examining opinions about conflict and typical conflict responses.

The Putnam-Wilson Conflict Styles Instrument (1982) measures three types of conflict styles: nonconfrontational, solution-oriented, and controlling. Users respond to thirty-five statements about conflict. The instrument attempts to control for the situation variable by instructing users to focus on a particular conflict they have encountered with peers in a task situation.

Focusing on the school setting, Kreidler (1984) articulates a system for categorizing approaches to conflict in the classroom. He identifies five basic approaches: the no-nonsense approach, the problem-solving approach, the compromising approach, the smoothing approach, and the ignoring approach. Each of these is stated briefly as a quasi philosophy for handling classroom conflicts. The no-nonsense approach, for example, is defined as "I don't give in. I try to be fair and honest with the kids, but they need firm guidance in learning what's acceptable behavior and what isn't." Kreidler also makes it clear that there is no single appropriate approach to conflict. Each approach has its appropriate uses; the goal is to understand which approaches one uses most often and to strengthen one's repertoire of responses.

From a different perspective, Augsberger (1973, p. 10) identifies concern for goals and concern for relationship as the two defining dimensions influencing conflict between two people who know each other. In his scheme there are five stances: I win, you lose; I walk away; I give in because of the relationship; I'll meet you halfway; and I'll hang in till we can both win. As with the other models, Augsberger stresses the importance of being able to use the full set of responses, and he notes that any one conflict may appropriately involve several different stances.

Despite the differences in these and other theoretical frameworks and in how they name conflict responses, there are significant similarities among them. Most use at least two dimensions of behavior in shaping their models (feelings and tasks, assertiveness and cooperation, concern for relationship and concern for goals). All stress the importance of being able to use all the responses. Although there is no single "right" response to conflict, there are responses that will be more effective and appropriate than others in a given conflict situation. The goal is to have a full repertoire of responses from which to choose and to know which response to use in a given situation.

Closely related to our conflict behaviors are our values, beliefs, and attitudes toward conflict. The next section explores basic orientations toward conflict that are often viewed as compatible with the field of conflict resolution.

Foundation, Values, Beliefs, and Self-Assessment Attitudes

Mary Parker Follett, one of the early advocates of conflict resolution in education, promoted an integrative approach to conflict resolution. One of her most significant achievements stemmed from her orientation toward service. Follett started the Community School Movement in Boston, a collaborative effort by people from diverse backgrounds to utilize school facilities as community centers.

In *Educating for a Peaceful World,* Morton Deutsch (1991), founder of the International Center for Cooperation and Conflict Resolution at Teachers College, Columbia University, and author of numerous studies and publications on conflict resolution, outlines the values, attitudes, and knowledge that foster constructive rather than destructive relations. These are the foundations of a peaceful environment. Deutsch proposes that foundational experiences in the interrelated areas of cooperative learning, conflict resolution, structured controversy, and school mediation must be at the core of any comprehensive effort to create a peaceful school environment. Corollaries to these experiences, according to Deutsch, include awareness of the causes and consequences of violence and of alternatives to violence, respect for self and others, avoidance of ethnocentrism and acceptance of the reality of cultural differences, and a view of conflicting interests as a mutual problem to be solved cooperatively. He further posits that "pervasive and extended experience in a school environment which provides daily experiences and modeling of cooperative relations and constructive resolution of conflicts, combined with tuition in the concepts and principles of cooperative work and conflict resolution, should enable students to develop generalizable attitudes and skills which will enable them, by the time they become adults, to cooperate with others in resolving constructively the inevitable conflicts that will occur among and within nations, ethnic groups, communities, and families" (p. 5).

In his book *Creative Conflict Resolution,* William Kreidler (1984), a spokesperson for the group Educators for Social Responsibility and a nationally recognized expert in school-based conflict resolution programs, sets forth several beliefs that underlie his approach to conflict resolution education. Kreidler states a belief that "adults and children can learn to resolve conflicts creatively and constructively, in ways that enhance both learning and interpersonal relationships" (p. 5). He further states that "teachers are capable of effectively dealing with conflict" (p. 5)—that they can be trusted to make the most important decisions about their own classrooms. Finally, he identifies the need for practical information and appropriate strategies that have proved effective in a variety of settings and for varying developmental and grade levels. Kreidler proposes that teachers are in a unique position, not only to see the effects of violence on children and their behavior, but also to do something about it—by teaching peacemaking skills.

The September 1992 issue of *Educational Leadership,* the journal of the Association for Supervision and Curriculum Development, was devoted to conflict resolution in education. In a lead article titled "Why We Must Teach Peace," Coleman McCarthy, a *Washington Post* columnist, founder of the Center for Teaching Peace, and teacher of a high school conflict resolution course in the Washington, D.C., area, eloquently explained why it is vital to teach conflict resolution in our schools: "Studying peace through nonviolence is as much about getting the bombs out of our hearts as it is about getting them out of the Pentagon budget. Every problem we have, every conflict, whether among our family or friends, or among governments, will be addressed either through violent force or nonviolent force. No third option exists. . . . I teach my classes because I believe in nonviolent force—the force of justice, the force of love, the force of sharing wealth, the force of ideas, the force of organized resistance to corrupt power" (p. 6).

McCarthy further proposed that, at present, it is very difficult to deal with conflict (in schools or anywhere else) through negotiation, compromise, or other nonviolent means, because those methods have never been consistently taught in school. "We don't know," he says, "because we weren't taught." The result of this academic neglect is "peace illiteracy . . . a land awash in violence"

(1992, p. 8). McCarthy has proposed that the Clinton administration establish a federal office of peace education, which could serve as a resource center for teaching conflict resolution skills in schools.

Another orientation toward conflict resolution that is specific to the education context is Kreidler's concept of the peaceable classroom (1984), an environment that possesses the following five qualities (p. 3):

1. *Cooperation.* Children learn to work together and trust, help, and share with each other.

2. *Communication.* Children learn to observe carefully, communicate accurately, and listen sensitively.

3. *Tolerance.* Children learn to respect and appreciate people's differences and to understand prejudice and how it works.

4. *Positive emotional expression.* Children learn to express feelings, particularly anger and frustration, in ways that are not aggressive or destructive, and children learn self-control.

5. *Conflict resolution.* Children learn the skills of responding creatively to conflict in the context of a supportive, caring community.

Source: From *Creative conflict resolution: More than 200 activities for keeping peace in the classroom* by William J. Kreidler. Copyright © 1984 by William J. Kreidler. Reprinted by permission of Scott, Foresman and Company.

In their book *Creating the Peaceful School*, Bodine, Crawford, and Schrumpf (1994) build upon Kreidler's concept, describing a vision of a peaceable school where two important goals exist: "First, the school becomes a more peaceful and productive environment where students and teachers together can focus on the real business of learning and having fun. Second, students and adults gain essential life skills that will benefit them not just in school, but also at home, in their neighborhood, and in their roles, present and future, as citizens in a democratic society" (p. 3).

Bodine, Crawford, and Schrumpf define the peaceful environment as one based on a philosophy that teaches nonviolence, compassion, trust, fairness, cooperation, respect, and tolerance. The pervasive theme in a peaceable school, which touches interactions among children, between children and adults, and among adults, is the valuing of human dignity and self-esteem. To build such a foundation in our schools, "All individuals must understand their human rights, respect those rights for self and others, and learn how to exercise their rights without infringing on the rights of others" (p. 17).

Deutsch; Kreidler; and Bodine, Crawford, and Schrumpf all build upon a long history of advocates for schoolwide transformation.

Thus, a comprehensive orientation toward conflict resolution in our schools includes not only questions of classroom method and curriculum content but also issues of whole-school climate and culture. A comprehensive approach to conflict resolution in the schools—that is, one that will impact school cultures and climate as well as academic achievement and individual behavior—must include programming that influences all members of the school family.

It is possible to pose—at least for consideration and discussion, if not definition—an initial list of values, beliefs, attitudes, and orientations that might be said to be compatible with the conflict resolution discipline. Distilled from the discussion above, that list might include positions espousing cooperation (as opposed to competition), nonviolence, compassion, trust, justice and fairness, respect for self and others, recognition, acceptance, celebration of differences, tolerance, effective and empathic communication, positive emotional expression, the definition of conflict as a mutual problem, a belief that people are capable of learning to resolve their own problems, and a belief that schools and teachers have a social responsibility to address issues of conflict and to teach conflict resolution skills.

Exploring the values, beliefs, and attitudes associated with conflict resolution requires not only thinking introspectively about the underlying motivations for choosing certain classroom methods and curricula but also examining one's own orientations and behaviors toward conflict. The maxim "Actions speak louder than words" reminds the conflict resolution educator to look inward as well as outward. Educators must clarify, both individually and within their professional community, the extent to which they are willing and able to "walk the talk."

The following questions about values, beliefs, and attitudes deserve reflection as well as collegial discussion:

- Are there prerequisite values, beliefs, and attitudes one must hold in order to be genuine in one's involvement with conflict resolution education?

- If so, what are those values, beliefs, and attitudes?

- Are there attitudes, beliefs, and behaviors that enhance or detract from a conflict resolution educator's effectiveness in his or her teaching, scholarship, and service to the discipline?

- Is it necessary, as a conflict resolution practitioner, to model particular values, beliefs, and attitudes outside of the classroom context? How important is that modeling?

- To what degree, if any, should a conflict resolution practitioner be an activist for social causes?

- Do the values, beliefs, and attitudes that underlie the discipline of conflict resolution transcend cultural differences?

Cultural Sensitivity

Conflict occurs in a context; so do our responses. Cultural factors form an important part of those contexts. These cultural elements include not only race, ethnicity, and religion but also gender, age, class, education, profession, sexual orientation, and physical ability. However, the complexity of the cultural factors in a given conflict extends beyond those separate elements brought by each party. First, there are dominant positions within any given culture (gender and age, for example). Second, there are dominant positions among cultures (in schools, for example, between English-speaking and Spanish-speaking cultures). Third, there are the disputants' family cultures, from which they have learned certain norms and expectations related to conflict behavior. Fourth, the setting in which the conflict occurs may have its own culture. Groups, organizations, institutions, neighborhoods, highways, sporting events, cities, regions—all involve formal or informal norms and expectations about behavior and, possibly, about how conflict is (or is not) to be expressed. Finally, all of these cultural elements interact intrapersonally and interpersonally.

For example, in a conflict over an empty bus seat, a young mother might feel that she is entitled to the seat by virtue of her gender but not by virtue of her age. The other party, an older man, might feel the tug within himself between his age entitlement and the demands of gender. Each party faces an intrapersonal struggle among cultural values, norms, and expectations; each must resolve this internal struggle and choose how to act in the situation at hand. Assuming that the woman settles on gender entitlement and the man on age entitlement, they will now experience an interpersonal struggle arising from these cultural cues. A resolution to this conflict may depend in part on the culture of the bus service, which may have an explicit policy reserving some seats for older passengers.

While some disputes are overtly and explicitly intercultural, all conflicts involve cultural differences to some degree. Therefore, being able to recognize one's own cultural cues and their influence is a first step toward building cultural sensitivity as a foundation for effective conflict resolution. The ability to acknowledge the cultural differences present in a conflict situation and to understand how these may influence the conflict and its resolution is the desired goal. The development of cultural sensitivity with respect to conflict does not require extensive studies on race, human development, or the great religions of the world. It does demand an openness to differences in goals, approaches, needs, feelings, and concerns—among various aspects of oneself as well as between oneself and the other party. It demands the use of communication skills to hear the real message.

Communication Skills

A major factor in the development of the conflict resolution discipline has been the Harvard Negotiation Project, founded by Roger Fisher and William Ury. Their landmark book *Getting to Yes*, first published in 1981 and updated with Bruce Patton in 1991, has gained acceptance in a variety of professions, including business and education, and has provided a springboard for applications of conflict resolution methods in a variety of settings and circumstances. In *Getting to Yes*, Fisher and Ury acknowledge that "without communication there is no negotiation," for "negotiation is a process of communicating" (p. 32).

According to Fisher and Ury, there are three big problems in communication. The first is that disputants may not actually be talking to each other in a way that can be understood. Frequently at least one participant has given up attempts to make things clear, and is instead *posturing:* talking to impress or convince others or to further cement her or his own position.

The second problem in communication is a problem of *attentiveness.* That is, even though the disputants may be talking to each other, neither may be hearing what the other is saying. The need for careful and attentive listening is obvious, yet communication studies have repeatedly shown that it is difficult to listen well, especially when the pressure of an ongoing negotiation is present.

The third problem of communication in the context of conflict resolution is that of *misunderstanding.* This is both a transmission and a reception problem. What one wants to communicate is rarely exactly what is communicated, and what is stated is often misinterpreted. When the communicators are themselves different in fundamental ways—that is, of different genders, cultures, or even languages—the chance of their misunderstanding each other is greatly increased.

In applying the principles of Fisher and Ury to the education setting, Bodine, Crawford, and Schrumpf (1994) clarify some essential basic skills that contribute to successful communication and that alleviate common communication problems. Those skills (and the accompanying behaviors) are as follows (adapted from Fisher, Ury, and Patton, 1991, pp. 34–36):

1. *Listening actively, not only to understand what is said but also to understand the speaker's perceptions, emotions, and context and to communicate back that he or she has been understood.* Behaviors encompassed in active listening include summarizing facts and feelings that have been heard, clarifying to confirm understanding, and adopting a physical posture of attentiveness (using nonverbal cues to convey an attitude of genuine respect and attentiveness).

2. *Speaking with the intent to be understood instead of with the intent to debate or impress.* Speaking with the sincere intent to be understood—in a clear, direct manner—is more likely to elicit a receptive response. Blaming, name-calling, or raising one's voice is, at the least, unproductive. Using toxic or value-laden language or presenting the problem in an either/or way or as a demand is likewise unadvisable. Behaviors that enhance speaking for understanding include framing the issue as a mutual problem with the potential to be creatively and mutually solved.

3. *Speaking about yourself instead of about the other.* It is more persuasive to describe a problem in terms of its impact on you than in terms of what the other side did or why you think they did it. Stating how you feel is difficult to challenge, and unlike a complaint or a criticism, it is less likely to force the other side to a defensive posture. The communication behavior utilized in this step is the use of "I" statements.

4. *Speaking for a purpose.* Before making a statement, the speaker needs to know what she wants the other to learn and understand, as well as what purpose this information might serve. Speaking for a purpose requires awareness and mutual understanding of assumptions, as well as mutual understanding of context and language. Speaking for a purpose means recognizing that some thoughts or disclosures are better left unsaid, not because one party will then be privy to information that can be used against the other but because they simply serve no productive purpose. Behaviors associated with speaking for a purpose include careful conflict analysis and self-evaluation.

5. *Adjusting for differences such as personality, gender, and culture.* There are many differences in communication styles and situations. Those differences—pacing, formality, physical proximity, bluntness of speaking, timing, the relationship between the parties, eye contact, and posture (to name a few)—influence what is said as well as what is understood. On the other hand, it is unwise to overgeneralize about an individual communication based on gender, culture, or any other difference. Individual differences exist within every group. Behaviors that help participants adjust for differences include seeking an understanding of cultural and ethnic diversity, to increase awareness of potential differences and their origins.

Self-evaluating biased and nonbiased behavior is also useful for monitoring strengths and weaknesses that can affect the conflict resolution process.

In the same way that communication skills enhance productive conflict resolution, other behaviors and actions inhibit and sabotage the resolution of conflict. Communication inhibitors include interrupting, judging, teasing, criticizing, offering advice, changing the subject, dominating the discussion, using deliberate deception, and refusing to negotiate. Communication inhibitors are often described as behaviors that escalate rather that de-escalate conflicts. Avoidance tactics, unnecessary competitiveness, threats, and violence are behaviors that make conflicts worse, not only reducing or eliminating any chance of resolution but also damaging both present relationships and the likelihood of positive interactions in the future.

Communicative, productive conflicts are characterized by cooperation between parties, more satisfying exchanges, and positive conceptions of the other's personality. Productive conflicts (that is, those that involve effective communication) leave the participants mutually satisfied and feeling as if they have gained something. As Hocker and Wilmot (1991) put it, "constructive communication sets the stage for productive conflict outcomes" (p. 39).

Dealing with Emotions

In almost any human interaction, emotions are likely to be present and to influence the course of events. According to Fisher, Ury, and Patton (1991), feelings are often more important than talk. Because emotions felt on one side will generate emotional responses on the other, acknowledging and understanding the role of emotions in the resolution of conflict is essential.

Emotions inform participants in a dispute about the importance of an issue to each side. According to Bolton (1979), when emotions are strong, dealing with the emotional aspects of conflict needs to happen first. Engaging in what Bolton calls a "structured exchange of the emotional aspects of the controversy" (p. 219) enables the participants to proceed to a rational and creative examination of the substantive issues that divide them. Emotional components of conflict include anger, distrust, defensiveness, scorn, resentment, fear, and rejection. Bolton further states that it is not enough to hear the others' emotions, they need also to be mutually understood and accepted.

Fisher, Ury, and Patton recommend several steps for dealing

effectively with emotions in the context of conflict situations. These include the following:

1. Recognize and understand the emotions of all involved, including your own.
2. Make your emotions explicit, and acknowledge them as legitimate.
3. Allow the other side to let off steam.
4. Do not react to emotional outbursts.

Following these guidelines assists conflict resolution in many ways. First, self-evaluating one's own emotional state and listening for a sense of how others feel provides an important dimension of understanding. A consideration of which factors are producing the observed emotions enhances a more holistic understanding of the problem. Second, making the feelings of each party a clear focus of discussion frees people from the burden of unexpressed emotions and replaces often inaccurate guessing and estimating about the emotions of others with accurate information. Acknowledging emotions as legitimate before moving on to work on the problem will actually free the parties to work on the problem more effectively. Third, helping others to express emotions provides important psychological release, making it easier to talk rationally later. Particularly when emotions are strong, participants need to vent their feelings. They need to both express their own emotions clearly and patiently listen to the expressions of others' emotions. Fourth, accepting and supporting behaviors will legitimatize the feelings expressed and actually help people self-regulate, because they realize there will be ample opportunity to express their feelings. The recommended behavior while the other participant is letting off steam is to listen without responding to attacks and to encourage complete disclosure of emotions until all has been expressed. Agreeing on a rule that only one person can express anger at a time makes it legitimate for others to listen and not respond in a manner that escalates the conflict.

Anger and effective means of dealing with it are particularly important in conflict situations. How we deal with our own and others' anger often determines whether a conflict is resolved to the satisfaction of all concerned. Mace and Mace (1976) suggest that there are two sides to constructive management of anger: responsible expression and helpful reception. Responsible expression means verbally naming and owning the emotion without attacking the other. Responsible expression seeks to understand the genuine stimulus for the anger being felt. Helpful reception—that is, the positive receiving of an expression of anger from another—means acknowledging the other person's feelings, gauging their intensity, and inviting the other to work jointly toward solutions. If expressed responsibly and helpfully received, anger can be constructive rather than destructive in conflict situations.

Lateral Thinking

Lateral thinking refers to an openness to consider and explore a wide variety of choices and potential solutions. It is a foundational skill for conflict resolution. A cooperative activity engaged in by all participants in a conflict, lateral thinking involves consideration of many options, creative generation of ideas, imagining consequences and potential outcomes, and ultimately the joint creation of a unique solution that respects the needs of all parties.

Fisher and Ury call this skill *creating options for mutual gain.* Creating new options involves

- Separating the act of inventing options from the act of judging them
- Broadening the apparent choices rather than looking for a single answer
- Searching for mutual gain
- Inventing ways to make decisions easier

Brainstorming is a key strategy for enabling lateral thinking. The purpose of brainstorming is to invent as many different ideas as possible to address the problem at hand. In a brainstorming session, participants are freed from criticism and judgment of their ideas. Brainstorming can be a productive way to generate options with individuals who share the same position. It can also be valuable when the activity engages all the parties to a dispute.

Broadening the choices means looking not for the "right" idea but for multiple ideas on which you might later build, providing room for negotiation. Broadening choices can occur when options are multiplied by moving between specific and general ideas. Viewing a conflict through different perspectives, such as the perspective of different professions and disciplines, provides another method for generating multiple options. Changing the strength, scope, and/or breadth of a proposal also increases the options. Reducing a problem to smaller, more manageable units with accompanying solutions, or enlarging the discussion to include broader, more far-reaching applications are both ways to increase choice.

Searching for mutual gains acknowledges the possibility— almost always present—of a win-win solution, the possibility of joint gain. Mutual gains often emerge from the identification of shared interests or from creatively dovetailing differing interests.

Finally, creative conflict resolvers need to make decisions as easy as possible for all the participants in a conflict. Evaluating options from the others' point of view and framing propositions to which a "yes" response can be easily solicited help to make conflict resolution easier for all concerned.

Establishing a solid context and developing foundational skills are prerequisite conditions for effective use of conflict resolution processes. The conflict resolution practitioner needs to identify, examine, evaluate, and nurture values, beliefs, and attitudes that enable effectiveness. Additionally, those engaged in conflict resolution need basic communication skills, effective ways to deal with emotions, and facility with creative thinking processes. To increase the likelihood of the transfer of productive conflict resolution education from teacher to student, educators must engage in building for themselves and with their students a clear set of foundational beliefs and values about conflict and its resolution, as well as a set of foundational skills. Understanding, practicing, and refining the basic skills of conflict resolution enables the framework processes into which those orientations and skills are set.

References

Augsberger, D. (1973). *The love fight: Caring enough to confront.* Scottsdale, PA: Herald Press.

Bodine, R. J., Crawford, D., & Schrumpf, F. (1994). *Creating the peaceful school.* Champaign, IL: Research Press.

Bolton, R. (1979). *People skills: How to assert yourself, listen to others, and resolve conflicts.* New York: Simon & Schuster.

Deutsch, M. (1991). *Educating for a peaceful world.* Amherst, MA: National Association for Mediation in Education Publication.

Fisher, R., Ury, W., and Patton, B. (1991). *Getting to yes: Negotiating agreement without giving in (second edition).* New York: Penguin Books.

Hocker, J., & Wilmot, W. (1991). *Interpersonal conflict* (3rd ed.). Dubuque, IA: W. C. Brown.

Kilmann, R., & Thomas, K. (1975). "Interpersonal conflict handling behavior as reflections of Jungian personality dimensions." *Psychology Reports, 37,* 971–980.

Kreidler, W. (1984). *Creative conflict resolution: More than 200 activities for keeping peace in the classroom.* Glenview, IL: Scott, Foresman.

Mace, D., & Mace, V. (1976). "Marriage enrichment: A preventive group approach for couples." In D.H.L. Olson (Ed.), *Treating relationships* (pp. 186–225). Lake Mills, IA: Graphic Publishing.

McCarthy, C. (1992, December 29). "Peace education: The time is now." *The Washington Post.*

McCarthy, C. (1992, September). "Why we must teach peace." *Educational Leadership*, pp. 6–9.

Putnam, L. L., & Wilson, C. E. (1982). "Communicative strategies in organizational conflicts: Reliability and validity of a measurement scale." In M. Burgoon (Ed.), *Communication yearbook 6*. Newbury Park, CA: Sage.

Exercises

The exercises in this module are designed to further clarify and provide experience in developing and enhancing the foundational orientations and skills of conflict resolution. This background will make it easier for individuals involved with education at all levels to manage conflict successfully, and it will help them develop a deeper understanding of the nature of conflict and its impact on the educational experience. Exercises 2.1 through 2.3 focus on self-assessment; Exercise 2.4 highlights values, attitudes, and beliefs; and Exercise 2.5 deals with cultural issues. Exercises 2.6 through 2.10 deal with communications, and Exercises 2.11 and 2.12 focus on emotions. Exercises 2.13 and 2.14 concern lateral thinking.

 Exercise 2.1. Conflict Styles in the Classroom

NOTE: This exercise helps students understand how prejudgment affects conflict.

Objectives

- Know one's personal attitudes, beliefs, and behaviors related to conflict
- Explore the concept of choosing beliefs, attitudes, and behaviors
- Identify the conflict behaviors one perceives as appropriate in school and classroom settings

Procedures

1. Give each participant a copy of Kreidler's questions on classroom conflict (Exhibit 2.1). Remind everyone that there are no right and wrong answers, that the purpose is to increase their awareness of personal behavior patterns.

2. Suggest that everyone think about specific conflicts. Those who are currently teaching or have recently taught can bring to mind the last several conflicts that occurred in their classroom. Those who have not yet had teaching experience can use examples from what they have observed and project how they might respond.

3. Direct each participant to complete the instrument and compute a total score for each category. Allow ten minutes for this.

4. Discuss the implications of the question sheet with the class. Review the meaning of each category the form presents (no-nonsense approach, problem-solving approach, compromising approach, smoothing approach, and ignoring approach), and find out which conflict resolution styles were dominant among the participants. What do the patterns look like?

5. Ask the participants to consider whether there are some areas in which they would like to score higher. Pose other useful questions: Why? Were there any surprises? When is each style useful? When can each style be inappropriate? Does the kind of conflict affect the type of response that is best?

Exhibit 2.1.   How Do You Respond to Conflict?

The following exercises are designed to help you take a closer look at how you respond to classroom conflicts. There are no trick questions and no absolutely right or wrong answers. The purpose of the exercise is not to open your behavior to judgment but simply to make you more aware of it.

Read the statements below. If a statement describes a response you usually make to classroom conflict, write *3* in the appropriate answer blank below. If it is a response you occasionally make, write *2* in the appropriate blank. If you rarely or never make that response, write *1*.

When there is a classroom conflict, I

1. Tell the kids to knock it off _____
2. Try to make everyone feel at ease _____
3. Help the kids understand one another's point of view _____
4. Separate the kids and keep them away from each other _____
5. Let the principal handle it _____
6. Decide who started it _____
7. Try to find out what the real problem is _____
8. Try to work out a compromise _____
9. Turn it into a joke _____
10. Tell them to stop making such a fuss over nothing _____
11. Make one kid give in and apologize _____
12. Encourage the kids to find alternative solutions _____
13. Help them decide what they can give on _____
14. Try to divert attention from the conflict _____
15. Let the kids fight it out, as long as no one gets hurt _____
16. Threaten to send the kids to the principal _____
17. Present the kids some alternatives from which to choose _____
18. Help everyone feel comfortable _____
19. Get everyone busy doing something else _____
20. Tell the kids to settle it on their own time, after school _____

I	II	III	IV	V
1 _____	2 _____	3 _____	4 _____	5 _____
6 _____	7 _____	8 _____	9 _____	10 _____
11 _____	12 _____	13 _____	14 _____	15 _____
16 _____	17 _____	18 _____	19 _____	20 _____
Totals _____	_____	_____	_____	_____

Now add the numbers in each column. Each column reflects a particular approach and attitude toward classroom conflict. In which column did you score highest? Find the appropriate number below and see if the description corresponds to your perception of your attitudes toward conflict.

I. The no-nonsense approach. I don't give in. I try to be fair and honest with the kids, but they need firm guidance in learning what's acceptable behavior and what isn't.

II. The problem-solving approach. If there's a conflict, there's a problem. Instead of battling the kids, I try to set up a situation in which we can all solve the problem together. This produces creative ideas and stronger solutions.

III. The compromising approach. I listen to the kids and help them listen to each other. Then I help them give a little. We can't all have everything we want. Half a loaf is better than none.

IV. The smoothing approach. I like things to stay calm and peaceful whenever possible. Most of the kids' conflicts are relatively unimportant, so I just direct their attention to other things.

V. The ignoring approach. I point out the limits and let the kids work things out for themselves. It's good for them, and they need to learn the consequences of their behavior. There's not a whole lot you can do about conflict situations anyway.

Source: From *Creative conflict resolution: More than 200 activities for keeping peace in the classroom K–6* by William J. Kreidler. Copyright © 1984 by William J. Kreidler. Reprinted by permission of Scott, Foresman and Company.

Exercise 2.2. Taking Stock

NOTE: This exercise helps students begin to think through how they currently deal with conflict, how their personal beliefs affect how they deal with conflict, and how their conflict styles might be affected by conflict resolution study.

Objectives

- Discover your personal attitudes, beliefs, and behaviors related to conflict
- Explore the concept of choosing beliefs, attitudes, and behaviors
- Identify the behaviors you perceive as appropriate in school and classroom settings

Procedures

1. Ask participants to list ten statements describing their behaviors related to handling conflict in the classroom. Give some examples to get the process started—something along the lines of "I sometimes ignore a not-too-disruptive conflict because of time" or "I prefer well-behaved students, but I never have any time to talk with them because the others get all my attention." Suggest that each person think about past experiences in the classroom. Ask those with teaching experience to think of specific conflicts or conflicts that occurred in the last week. For those who have only observed in classrooms and have not worked directly with children, ask them to recall conflicts they have seen and to project the behavior they would be likely to exhibit. Allow five to ten minutes for this.

2. Ask participants to list ten statements describing their behaviors related to conflict with peers or colleagues. Again, suggest that each person bring memories of real conflicts to mind. Allow five minutes for this.

3. Ask participants to review their twenty statements in the context of the models for analyzing and categorizing conflict responses. Then ask them to summarize their conflict style by completing the statements given in Exhibit 2.2. Allow twenty minutes for this.

4. In groups of three or four (or in the large group), ask participants to share what they learned about their conflict style from completing the personal conflict style assessment. Allow fifteen minutes for this step.

Exhibit 2.2. Personal Conflict Style Assessment

Review the twenty statements you have chosen to describe your response to conflict in the classroom and with peers. Then complete the following statements:

1. In general, I would say I have chosen a response style that could be

   described as _____

2. I think I am best at handling conflicts that concern _____

   _____

3. I am often less effective at handling conflicts that concern _____

   _____

4. The most helpful skills I bring to conflicts are _____

   _____

5. My conflict responses would be more effective if I had better skills in

   _____

Exercise 2.3. Responding to Conflict

NOTE: This exercise flows from the previous one. It expands students' discussion about behavior, traditional school responses to "bad" behavior, conflict, and conflict resolution.

Objective

- Identify the behaviors you perceive to be appropriate in educational settings

Procedures

1. Pass out Exhibit 2.3, which presents a variety of different types of conflicts. Ask the participants to make notes on each case, indicating what they would do in the circumstances faced by the highlighted party in the conflict.

2. Select one conflict scenario, and discuss it with the whole group to model the kinds of analysis and discussion that might be helpful. Remind participants of the different models for extending thinking about what a conflict is about. Remind participants about the value of different responses and approaches in different situations.

3. Have the class form groups of three to five to discuss the conflict scenarios that raised the most questions for each group member.

4. Reassemble the class and have the groups and individuals report on what they learned from the exercise.

Exhibit 2.3. Responding to Conflict Worksheet

For each of the conflict scenarios below, decide what the person identified by boldface print should do next. Questions to consider include the following: What is this conflict about? Who needs to be involved? Should this conflict be dealt with through direct action or intervention? Is negotiation or mediation appropriate? Would a consensus process be appropriate?

1. A white student has a person of color for an **instructor**. This student mimics the instructor's speech during class. The instructor has an accent but speaks English proficiently. This occurs several times during class meetings.

2. An African American student is called "nigger" by a European American student who was upset with the African American student. The **classroom teacher** makes the student apologize for name-calling and requires the student to complete an assignment on prejudice. Two African American students are talking. One student responds, "Okay, nigger. I got your number." The white student overhears the comment, as does the classroom teacher. The two African American students continue their conversation.

3. Ricky and Joe are among several elementary school students playing on the slide during recess. Both boys know about the school rule allowing only one person at a time on the slide. Ricky sits on the top of the slide, joking that he is "King of the Mountain" and will not come down. Joe, a relatively new student, calls Ricky a derogatory term. The **recess teacher** sees Ricky and Joe fighting at the foot of the slide.

4. A professor has an idea for a research project and gives it to a **doctoral student**. Later on, the faculty member decides to participate more actively in the research. Upon completing an article on the research, the faculty member does not list the student as an author, but rather gives an "acknowledgment" to the student.

5. A group of students at a high school indicate that they want to include a prayer in their graduation ceremony. The **principal** receives a petition signed by over 90 percent of the graduating class. An outside group opposing prayer in school objects to this.

6. A **parent** comes to see her child's teacher about the teacher's perceptions of her child. The teacher thinks the child misbehaves. The parent feels the child has never done anything wrong.

7. A professor assigns a student exercise requiring teamwork and consensus building. The end product of the assignment is to be a group presentation. It is planned as a major part of the course grade. The **students** on one team are unable to get a team member to cooperate in preparing the project. The students get a C+ because that one team member gives a very poor and lengthy presentation.

8. A fifth-grade student is told by her **teacher** to quit talking and sit down. The student tells the teacher to "shut up!" and refuses to sit down. The rest of the class looks on in total silence.

Exercise 2.4. Clarifying Orientations Toward Conflict Resolution

NOTE: This exercise encourages the student to review, think about, and discuss the substance of the background material in this module.

Objectives

- Identify values, beliefs, and attitudes associated with conflict resolution

- Examine your own orientations toward conflict resolution, identifying attitudes and beliefs that may enable or disable your future effectiveness as a conflict resolution practitioner

Procedures

1. Lead the full class in a discussion of the way values, beliefs, and attitudes can influence conflict resolution. Ask participants to volunteer informal definitions of what values, beliefs, and attitudes are. (It is not necessary, for the purposes of this discussion, to clearly discriminate between the three areas.) Use the points covered in the Background section of the module to enrich the discussion, as needed.

2. Pose this question to the class: Are specific values, beliefs, and attitudes essential to the discipline of conflict resolution?

3. Ask each participant to take a few minutes to write down on an index card any values, beliefs, and attitudes that seem to be essential.

4. Direct participants to pair up with someone they do not know and compare lists. Instruct the partners to identify similarities and differences on their lists. For every difference, each partner should explain why that particular issue appears essential.

5. Have the partners then compile a joint list that includes all the items named. Items common to both lists should be underlined on the new list.

6. Have the partners pair up into groups of four. Ask each pair to share their joint list with the other pair. Have them again discuss similarities and differences between lists.

7. Have the foursome draft a composite list on chart paper, indicating to the left of each item the number of participants (from one to four) who listed that particular item.

8. Reassemble the class. Have the foursomes share their lists with the whole group, noting the similarities and differences on the individual lists. It may be useful to compile a composite list on

chart paper and post it for future reference. The following process questions can be used to enrich the general discussion:

   a. Are there prerequisite values, beliefs, and attitudes one must hold in order to be genuine in one's involvement with conflict resolution education?

   b. What, if any, are those values, beliefs, and attitudes?

   c. What attitudes, beliefs, and behaviors might enhance or detract from a conflict resolution educators' effectiveness in teaching, scholarship, and service to the discipline? (The instructor might suggest that students think about fairness, respect for others, appreciation of differences, and tolerance.)

   d. Is it necessary, as a conflict resolution practitioner, to model particular values, beliefs, or attitudes outside of the classroom context? How important is that modeling?

   e. To what degree should a conflict resolution practitioner be an activist? (*Activist* here refers to someone who works on behalf of social causes such as freedom of expression, human rights, racial equality, gender equity, gun control, peace, and nonviolence.)

   f. Do the values, beliefs, and attitudes that underlie the discipline of conflict resolution transcend cultural differences?

Alternative Procedure

1. Assemble the whole class, and pose questions a, d, e, and f from step 8 of the primary procedure.

2. For each question, invite participants to stand and take a position on a "continuum line" extending across the front of the meeting room. Explain that one endpoint represents a position of strong agreement and the other a position of strong disagreement. (Note that questions b and c are eliminated in this alternative exercise. They might be used as a basis for a more detailed discussion of the points of the exercise during a debriefing.)

3. Once all the participants have taken a position on a question, interview individuals at random concerning why they have chosen to stand at that point on the continuum.

Assignment (Optional)

Ask participants to assess their own values, beliefs, and attitudes on conflict and conflict resolution and to consider how those factors might influence their effectiveness in dealing with conflict.

Suggest or request that participants write up their conclusions regarding their self-assessment and steps that could be taken to make changes, if changes seem warranted. You can either have participants keep the resulting papers themselves, as a benchmark of their approach to conflict resolution at this point in the training, or turn them in so that you will be able to see where they are. If you do read the papers, keep the contents confidential, thus allowing participants to reveal their views or not as they see fit.

 ## Exercise 2.5. Culture and Conflict

NOTE: This exercise is intended to help students think through the broadest meaning of culture that they can.

Objectives

- Know your personal attitudes, beliefs, and behaviors related to conflict
- Understand the influence of culture on conflict behavior

Procedures

1. Review with participants some basic concepts related to culture. The definition of culture provided in Module One could be introduced or reintroduced here. It may also be helpful to provide definitions of race and ethnicity and to show the relationships between all three terms. Participants may have some confusion about terms—culture, subculture, bicultural—and about the notion of primary and secondary cultural identifications. Since discussions of culture often trigger some anxiety, remind participants that the purpose of the exercise is to help develop personal understanding, not to judge ourselves or others.

2. Ask participants to complete the questionnaire in Exhibit 2.4, which addresses their personal cultural identity and their cultural, family, and professional norms for expressing and resolving conflict.

3. Divide participants into small groups to discuss how they think their culture affects their conflict behaviors. Do people from the same culture find similar effects?

4. In the large group, share insights and identify remaining questions about culture and conflict.

Exhibit 2.4. Culture and Conflict Questionnaire

1. From what culture do you draw your primary identity?
2. Do you belong to other cultural groups that play significant roles in shaping who you are? List them here, but answer the rest of the questions from the point of view of your primary group.
3. In what ways has the group with which you have a primary identification been an asset to you?
4. Are there ways in which identification with your primary culture has created difficulties or problems for you? Describe them briefly.
5. Do people make assumptions about your culture that positively or negatively affect you? What are they?
6. In what circumstances does your primary cultural identification create comfort for others?
7. In what circumstances does your primary cultural identification create discomfort for others?
8. What other cultures are you most comfortable with? Why?
9. With what other cultures are you least comfortable? Why?

For the next group of questions, please think back to a conflict you had with an individual or group with a different primary cultural identification.

10. In what ways did your approach to the conflict reflect the values, beliefs, or norms of your culture?
11. In what ways did your approach to the conflict depart from the values, beliefs, or norms of your primary culture?
12. In what ways did your approach to the conflict reflect the values and norms of your family beliefs?
13. In what ways did your approach to the conflict depart from the values and norms of your family beliefs?
14. In what ways did cultural differences affect how you approached the conflict?
15. What have you learned from conflicts with people from other cultural groups?
16. Are there some groups with whom you find communicating, in general, more comfortable? Are there some with whom you find communicating less comfortable? Describe briefly.

For the next three questions, please think about some recent conflicts at your educational institution.

17. What cultural groups are dominant at your institution? Which is dominant in terms of numbers? Which is dominant in terms of influence? At which levels?
18. How would you describe the culture of your institution?
19. What values or norms do you see reflected in recent conflicts at your institution?
20. What questions do you have about culture and conflict?

Adapted from Jim Halligan (Community Board Program, Inc.) and Marsha Peterzell (Wilson High School, San Francisco Unified School District), 1989.

Exercise 2.6. Active Listening Techniques

NOTE: Active listening is a communication technique essential for productive conflict resolution. An active listener uses nonverbal behaviors (such as eye contact and gestures) as well as verbal behaviors (tone of voice, open-ended questioning, restating, summarizing) to demonstrate to the speaker that he or she is paying attention.

Objective

- Identify and enhance communication skills that will improve conflict resolution processes

Procedures

1. Hand out a copy of Exhibit 2.5, "Are You an Effective Communicator?" to each participant.

2. Ask participants to pair off for this exercise. Have the pairs sit facing each other and decide who will speak and who will listen first. (Note that everyone will have a chance to take both roles.)

3. Outline the procedure as follows. The speaker will choose an issue and talk for about five minutes. During this time, the listener should exhibit as many active listening behaviors as possible. Active listening techniques practiced here can include nonverbal behaviors like leaning forward, making eye contact, and nodding. The listener may also encourage, clarify, restate, summarize, reflect, and validate.

4. After five minutes, tell the partners to switch roles.

5. After another five minutes, stop the exercise and give participants a few minutes to complete the checklist, each for her or his own listening behavior.

6. Have the pairs discuss their responses to the checklist with each other, giving examples of active listening behaviors and discussing what was easy and difficult about the activity.

7. Pose the following process questions to enrich the discussion:

   a. Of the active listening techniques listed in the questionnaire, which ones did you do or not do?

   b. What was easy about this exercise?

   c. What was difficult about this exercise? What barriers to active listening did you identify?

    d. What is an example (that you used) of an encouraging statement? a clarifying statement? a restating statement? a reflecting statement? a validating statement?

    e. What are the cultural implications of active listening techniques as they have been described in this exercise? (For example, do all cultures regard eye contact as positive?)

Exhibit 2.5.   Are You an Effective Communicator?

Use this checklist to evaluate your communication skills.

	Yes	No	Sometimes
1. Do you make eye contact?	☐	☐	☐
2. Do you watch the person's body posture and facial expressions?	☐	☐	☐
3. Do you empathize and try to understand the person's feelings, thoughts, and actions?	☐	☐	☐
4. Do you keep from interrupting and let the person finish, even though you already know what the person means?	☐	☐	☐
5. Do you ask questions to clarify information?	☐	☐	☐
6. Do you smile and nod your head to show interest?	☐	☐	☐
7. Do you listen, even if you do not like the person who is talking or what the person is saying?	☐	☐	☐
8. Do you ignore outside distraction?	☐	☐	☐
9. Do you listen for and remember important points?	☐	☐	☐
10. Do you keep from judging what was said (do you remain neutral)?	☐	☐	☐

Source: From *Peer mediation conflict resolution in schools* (Program Guide, p. 55) by F. Schrumpf, D. Crawford, and H. C. Usadel, 1991, Champaign, IL: Research Press. Copyright 1991 by the authors. Reprinted by permission.

Exercise 2.7. Clarifying Meaning with Open-Ended Questions

NOTE: Another aspect of active listening involves clarifying meaning to get additional information and making sure you understand the other side's needs and interests. Open-ended questions (that is, questions that cannot be answered with a simple yes or no) elicit more information and help establish your impartiality as a listener. Some examples of open-ended questions are

- Can you tell me more about [whatever]?
- What happened next?
- How did you feel about that?

This exercise consists of two segments, one designed to illustrate the value of open-ended questions and the other to allow the group to practice using such questions.

Objective

- Identify and enhance communication skills that will improve conflict resolution processes

Procedures (Value)

1. Tell the group that you are going to play a variant of "twenty questions," with no limit on the number of questions. You have a particular person in mind, and the group's task is to come up with that person's name. As in twenty questions, group members can ask only closed-ended (yes or no) questions.

2. Call for questions and answer them, with yes or no, until the group discovers the identity of the person you are thinking of. Make tally marks on chart paper or a blackboard to keep track of the number of questions required.

3. Now tell the group that for the next round the game will be the opposite of twenty questions. They still have to figure out who you have in mind, but this time they can ask only open-ended questions—that is, questions that are impossible to answer responsively with a simple yes or no.

4. Go through another question-and-answer session until the group discovers the new name. Keep a tally, as before, of the number of questions required.

5. Ask the following discussion questions to help the class analyze the exercise:

a. Which method required more questions? Why?

b. Which method elicited more information? Why?

c. Which form of communication was more comfortable? Why?

d. Which method was more effective? Why?

Procedures (Practice)

1. Have participants assemble in groups of five. In each group, ask for one volunteer who is willing to briefly describe a current professional problem. Advise the speakers to keep their explanations down to a few sentences, withholding information in anticipation of the questioning to follow.

2. Ask the other participants in each small group to try to gain a more complete picture of the situation by asking the speaker open-ended questions. Have a second volunteer in each group note the initiating phrase of each question on chart paper (for example, "Can you tell us more about—").

3. Allow about ten minutes, then reassemble the class and post all the charts of initiating phrases where everyone can see them.

4. Have the group discuss the exercise. Work the following process questions into the discussion:

a. What was this experience like for the speaker? for the listener?

b. What were the most helpful starting phrases?

c. What else can you do to enhance your skill in asking open-ended questions?

Exercise 2.8. Summarizing

NOTE: Summarizing, another essential aspect of active listening, means restating facts you have heard by repeating the most important points and discarding extra information. Summarizing also includes reflecting on feelings you have observed. Summarizing permits a review of progress, offers a chance to pull together ideas and facts, and establishes a basis for more discussion.

Objective

- Identify and enhance communication skills that will improve conflict resolution processes

Procedures

1. Have participants form into groups of three, consisting of a speaker, a listener, and an observer. (Warn the groups to choose speakers willing to describe problems they have experienced, are experiencing, or have observed in the educational environment.)

2. Outline the following roles:

   a. Speaker: Spend a few minutes describing the problem.

   b. Listener: Listen actively, preparing to summarize and restate facts and reflect feelings.

   c. Observer: Observe the interaction and prepare to comment on it.

3. Allow about three minutes, then ask the triads to consider these process questions:

   a. To the listener: Was it difficult to summarize both facts and feelings accurately?

   b. To the speaker: Did the listener accurately summarize the information? How did the listener show understanding of your feelings?

   c. To the observer: What did you observe? Did the listener organize the interests of the other? Did the listener repeat the most important points (and so on)?

4. If time allows, have the members of the triads switch roles and repeat the exercise.

Exercise 2.9. Reframing

NOTE: Reframing is the process of using language to alter the way each person or party in a conflict conceptualizes attitudes, behaviors, issues, and interests or defines the situation. By putting things in more neutral terms, reframing can help alleviate defensiveness, increase understanding, and reduce tension. Reframing can soften demands, identify underlying interests, and remove emotions and value-laden language from communications. When engaging in reframing, it is essential to keep in mind that every assertion has a kernel of truth and has relevance for the person who makes it. The purpose of reframing is to open doors to communication, not to discount anyone's feelings or interests.

Reframing can involve:

- Changing the person who communicates the message
- Changing the syntax or wording of the message
- Changing the meaning of a statement by broadening or narrowing the meaning and focusing away from positions and toward interests
- Changing the context of the situation by identifying common ground and minimizing differences

Objective

- Identify and enhance communication skills that will improve conflict resolution processes

Procedures

1. Have participants form new groups of three.

2. Hand out one copy of Exhibit 2.6, "Reframing Exercise," to each group.

3. Ask the groups to take each statement on the list and reframe it in one of the ways you have described, with a view to promoting more positive communication. Someone in each group should record the reframed statements in the spaces provided on the form.

4. Reassemble the class and ask participants to share their reframed statements. Use the following process questions to enrich the discussion:

a. What was easy or difficult about this exercise?

b. What approaches to reframing were helpful to you?

  c. What general conclusions can be drawn from this exercise? *Note:* Make sure these insights emerge from the discussion.

Statements that begin with "you" put people on the defensive. Words like "always" and "never" tend to escalate a situation. Problem statements make very useful frames for issues. (Use starters like "How can we—" and "What can we do to—" to engage the listener's mind in working on the problem rather than fighting with the speaker.)

Discussion is most productive when

- Statements focus on the problem, not the people involved.
- Statements avoid threatening basic needs of individuals or groups.
- Statements are as brief and concise as possible.
- Statements allow for the possibility of more than one solution to the problem.

Exhibit 2.6. Reframing Exercise

For each of the following sentences, reframe the statement in a more positive light.

1. You never pay attention to what anyone else thinks!

   _____

   _____

2. You always seem to get out of doing the work that the rest of us have to do!

   _____

   _____

3. You make me sick!

   _____

   _____

4. I want this assignment on my desk by tomorrow morning or else!

   _____

   _____

5. You are unfair!

   _____

   _____

6. Sit down and shut up!

   _____

   _____

7. You'll do what I say or else!

   _____

   _____

8. This is the worst version of this assignment that I have ever seen! How did you get admitted to this university?

   _____

   _____

9. Just once I'd like to see you show up on time for a department meeting!

_____

_____

10. You're a bigot!

_____

_____

Exercise 2.10. Improving Communication Using "I" Messages

NOTE: One of the challenges of communication is to speak in a way that can be accurately understood by the listener. This requires conveying not only facts about the situation but also feelings. Three-part "I" messages provide one framework for communicating both meaning and emotion. An "I" message focuses attention on the speaker instead of the listener and allows the speaker to express interests and needs in an assertive but nonthreatening way. The choice of whether or not to use "I" messages must be considered, like all communication, in the context of culture, since the method is not equally accepted in all cultures. The formula for "I" messages may feel contrived at first, but when employed often, it becomes a very natural and effective communication strategy.

> An "I" message consists of three parts:
> I feel _____ (emotional response)
> when _____ (something happens, somebody does something)
> because _____ (reason).

> Sometimes it is useful to add a fourth phrase:
> and I need _____ (corrective action).

For example: I feel *angry* when I get home and find dirty dishes, because *I'm the only one who does the dishes, and I'm tired.* I need *a way to share this chore with you.*

Objective

- Identify and enhance communication skills that will improve conflict resolution processes.

Procedures

1. Ask participants to form groups of four and sit in a circle (preferably around a table).

2. Give each participant one blank sheet of paper.

3. Ask each participant to write a one-sentence description of a problem at the top of the page, using the present tense and the second person. (For example, "When you arrive back at your office after class, you find that your office roommate has left the door open and the room unattended." Or, "You find a colleague's car in your assigned parking space; this is the third time this week the same colleague has done this.") Allow about twenty minutes for this activity.

4. Have all the participants pass their papers to the right, so that everyone has someone else's problem description.

5. Ask each participant to design an appropriate "I" message addressing the problem described on the page and to write the "I" message immediately below the problem statement. Allow about five minutes for this activity.

6. Have all the participants pass their papers to the right again, and repeat steps 3 to 5 using the other side of the paper.

7. Reassemble the class and review several problem statements and accompanying "I" messages. Pass the papers one more time to the right, so that everyone has a sheet that includes "I" messages written by someone else. Then call for volunteers to read off the ones they find most interesting and effective.

8. Use the following process questions to enrich the discussion:

    a. What was easy or difficult about this exercise?

    b. Are there situations in which making "I" statements might be more difficult? When and why?

    c. Can "I" messages be used in appreciative ways? How?

    d. During the course of a conflict, when might an "I" message be helpful?

    e. How might "I" messages help to prevent conflict?

Note: If a substantial proportion of the group seems to find this exercise difficult, repeat it in different foursomes to give the participants more practice.

 ### Exercise 2.11. Analyzing Anger

NOTE: How we deal with both our own anger and the anger of others often determines whether a conflict is resolved successfully or escalates to a more serious level. It is important to realize that anger is a secondary emotion. Behind all anger is fear. The fear-anger progression means (1) a threat is perceived, (2) fear is stimulated, and (3) anger is expressed. A first step in the responsible expression of anger is to identify the underlying fear. The underlying fear is the cause of the emotion. Understanding the cause of fear provides the possibility to reduce fear, allowing for more successful communication and collaboration.

Objective

- Identify and enhance communication skills that will improve conflict resolution processes.

Procedures

1. Invite several faculty members or other individuals to join this class session and serve as facilitators. (Try to find one facilitator for every eight participants in the class.) Brief each one in advance on the content of the exercise and the facilitator's role in it. Facilitators with conflict resolution training are preferred but not essential. They must be able to lead the discussion and have some practice with this exercise and the next one in advance of presenting the lessons.

2. Ask the class to assemble into groups of eight participants and one facilitator. Have each group sit in a circle with an easel and chart paper nearby. You may wish to hand out written instructions for steps 3 to 5 rather than (or in addition to) explaining the task orally.

3. Instruct the participants to generate a list of between eight and twenty situations in which they have experienced anger. The group facilitator then lists the situations in the form of phrases on the chart paper.

4. Direct the groups to return to the top of their lists and attempt as a group to identify fears that could underlie the anger in each situation. Warn participants to keep in mind that each of the situations is real to a group member. After discussing possibilities, the facilitator should ask the owner of the situation what the underlying fear might be.

5. After several anger situations have been discussed, ask group members to look for common themes or fears that were experienced. Make sure the facilitators stress the idea that the first step in anger management is understanding your own fears and the fears of others.

 ## Exercise 2.12. Managing Anger

NOTE: Anger is a particularly important emotion in conflict situations. Learning to control anger is an essential step in managing conflict. Instructors should be confident of their own ability to handle this exercise before attempting it, or they should obtain the assistance of a professional who is.

Objective

- Identify and enhance communication skills that will improve conflict resolution processes.

Procedures

1. Ask participants to pair off, sit facing each other, and decide who will speak and who will listen first.

2. Direct the listeners to practice active listening techniques, being as fully present and attentive as possible.

3. Ask the speakers to bring to mind a situation that made them angry. Direct them to describe the situation to their listeners with as much feeling as possible, allowing the feelings of anger to surface.

4. Allow the speakers one or two minutes for the descriptions, then call out "Stop! Breathe slowly for a few minutes!"

5. Allow another minute or two for the group to cool down, then direct the participants to switch roles, with the new listener discarding the anger recently felt and focusing completely upon the situation being described.

6. After one or two minutes, call out "Stop! Breathe slowly for a few minutes!" and have the participants switch roles again. Direct the original speaker to continue with the first conflict account, recapturing and expressing the anger it evoked.

7. Repeat steps 3 to 6 several times, with the second speaker also continuing with the scenario he or she originally chose. This process allows each participant to become accustomed to picking up anger and setting it aside again. Go through the process at least two times (as many as four times if time allows).

8. Reassemble the class and invite the participants to talk about the exercise. Use the following process questions to enrich the discussion:

    a. What was easy/difficult about this exercise?

    b. What did this exercise tell you about controlling anger?

Make sure the discussion covers the fact that anger can be controlled, that specific actions help to alleviate anger responses, and that anger causes physical symptoms.

Exercise 2.13. Problem-Solving Challenges

NOTE: The term *lateral thinking* refers to an openness to explore a wide variety of potential solutions. It requires unconventional approaches and a willingness to look at a problem from different points of view. In conflict resolution, lateral thinking helps the disputants create options for mutual gain, broadening their range choices beyond what may at first seem apparent. The following exercise offers several experiences in lateral thinking.

Objective

- Identify and enhance thinking skills that will improve conflict resolution processes

Procedure 1. Blue Line

1. Before the exercise begins, lay out blue ribbons about twenty-four inches on the floor long to make straight lines in various locations in the room. You need one ribbon for each pair of participants.

2. Ask the participants to pair off and take positions on either side of a blue line (that is, with one partner standing on one side of the line and one on the other side).

3. Tell participants to find some way to get the person across from them to come over to their side. They may use any means or ideas that come to mind. (*Note:* Caution participants that you're going to call time in a few minutes, and they must remain in whatever position they find themselves in at that moment.)

4. Call "Begin."

5. Allow one or two minutes, then call "Freeze!" and direct participants to remain in position during the discussion to follow.

6. Go over the exercise with the group, using the following process questions to enrich the discussion:

   a. What methods did you use in attempting to reach your goal?

   b. How effective were you?

   c. Is there any way for both people to reach the goal? (Often one group has determined that they need only to change places to have both goals accomplished.)

7. Have one pair demonstrate a win-lose solution (one person has come over to the other person's side); a lose-lose situation (no movement has taken place); and a win-win solution (change places). Then ask participants these questions:

a. Why don't most people think of changing places? (*Note:* The answers to this question and the one following will vary, but they will likely illustrate our largely common cultural bias toward win-lose solutions.)

b. What does this exercise tell us about conflict resolution?

Procedure 2. Nine Dots

1. Have the group sit at tables. Distribute Exhibit 2.7 to each participant.

2. Direct participants to place the point of their pen on any dot and then attempt to connect all the dots, using no more than four straight lines and without picking the pen up from the paper.

3. After a few minutes, invite someone who has discovered a way to accomplish the task to come forward and demonstrate the solution on chart paper. If no one has discovered a solution, invite participants to form partnerships to work on a solution together for a few minutes.

4. If no one discovers a solution, illustrate the answer.

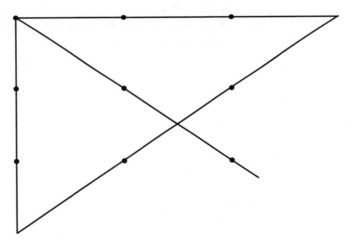

Figure 2.1. Solution to Nine Dots Exercise.

5. Go over the exercise with the group, using the following process questions to enrich the discussion:

a. If you had difficulty discovering the answer, what were the barriers that limited your exploration?

b. If you discovered the answer, what thinking steps did you follow?

c. How did you feel if others discovered a solution before you did?

d. What does this exercise have to do with conflict resolution? *Note:* This exercise is a common way to illustrate linear thinking. It tests participants' ability to use lateral thinking to find a solution.

Procedure 3. The Eighteenth Camel

1. Assemble the class and tell this story.

A father had 17 camels. When he died, his will left the 17 camels to his three sons, in the following way: the eldest was to receive half of the camels, the middle son one-third of the camels, and the youngest son one-ninth of the camels. The three sons thought and figured, but they could discern no way to satisfy their father's wishes. So they decided to take their problem to the Wise Woman. When they explained their difficulty, the Wise Woman said, "I have 1 camel, which you may use. Add that one to your 17 camels. With 18 camels you can now give the oldest son 9 camels, the middle son 6 camels, and the youngest son 2 camels. Then give me my camel back, and all will be as your father wished."

2. Discuss the story with the group, asking them to explain what it has to do with resolving conflict. (The moral of the story is that sometimes, in creating a solution, you need to look for that eighteenth camel.)

Exhibit 2.7. Nine Dots

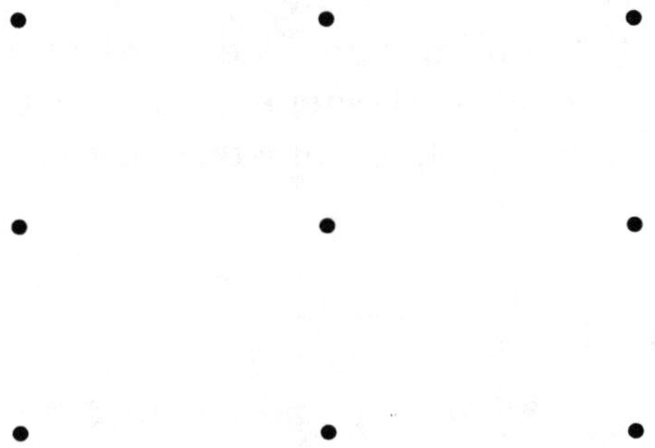

Exercise 2.14. Brainstorming

NOTE: Brainstorming is a foundational activity for creating options for mutual gain. The word literally means a "storm of ideas." By separating the generation of ideas from assessing or choosing solutions, we free ourselves to think more creatively and broaden our choices.

Objectives

- Identify and enhance thinking skills that will improve conflict resolution processes
- Examine and apply the foundational orientations and skills of conflict resolution in the context of the educational environment

Procedure 1. Marshmallow Storm

1. Introduce the exercise, acknowledging that most people are already familiar with the brainstorming technique.

2. Give each participant a copy of Exhibit 2.8, which recaps the rules for brainstorming.

3. Have the participants assemble in groups of five or six. Give each group a sheet of chart paper and a marker.

4. Display a bag of marshmallows. Ask the groups to brainstorm at least twenty ideas for using the bag of marshmallows. (Remind the participants of the rules of brainstorming and request that everyone monitor the rules as the discussion proceeds.)

5. Ask one group to share their list with the class. Ask the remaining groups to add any ideas not on the first group's list.

6. Briefly discuss some of the most creative ideas for using the marshmallows, helping the group see how brainstorming contributed to the creation of ideas.

Procedure 2. Intercultural Case Study

1. Give each work group a copy of the Intercultural Case Study in Appendix C. (This case study can be used in different ways to support exercises throughout the manual.)

2. Select one of the conflicts in the Intercultural Case Study in advance of the lesson and instruct each group to brainstorm as many ideas as possible to help solve the problem at hand. Have a volunteer within each group record the group's ideas on chart paper.

3. Ask the groups, one at a time, to describe the ideas they came up with. After each group shares their ideas, ask the class as a whole for other ideas that may have been stimulated by what was just heard.

4. Go over the exercise with the group, using the following process questions to enrich the discussion:

     a. Which ideas seem to provide mutual gain?

     b. Which ideas are most creative?

     c. Did anyone withhold an idea? Why?

     d. Was judgment withheld in the groups?

     e. Did anyone build upon someone else's idea to create a related one?

     f. What cultural/ethnic/gender factors need to be considered when using the brainstorming technique?

Exhibit 2.8.   Rules for Brainstorming

- Say any idea that comes to mind. Don't censor your thoughts—blurt out ideas.
- Do not judge or discuss ideas. Accept all ideas at this time—no criticizing.
- Come up with as many ideas as possible. If you get stuck, offer variants on ideas already stated.
- Try to think of unusual, strange, bizarre, far-out suggestions. Sometimes these will help others to think of new practical possibilities.

Alternative Dispute Resolution Processes

Alternative dispute resolution includes a spectrum of processes that employ communication skills and creative thinking to develop voluntary solutions acceptable to those concerned in a dispute. Unlike avoidance or aggressive responses to conflict, this approach enables not only more creative and mutually satisfying agreements but also the maintenance and improvement of relationships between and among persons who initially disagree.

This module introduces the various forms of alternative dispute resolution. The basic process of negotiation is then examined in more depth. Negotiation is the foundational procedure of conflict resolution. It provides the underlying principles and practices for mediation and consensus building, which are also discussed in the Background section.

The fundamental assumption of this module is that conflict resolution processes—negotiation, mediation, and consensus building—need to be studied, observed, modeled, and practiced before they can be effectively utilized. Particularly for educators who are incorporating the processes into teaching and other educational activities, a firm understanding of methods of conflict resolution and a high level of skill in conducting those processes is essential.

The overall goal of this module is to engage the participants in exercises and simulations that will begin to develop their understanding of these concepts and their skill in applying them. The module is not designed to provide the comprehensive training needed to function as a formal professional negotiator or mediator.

Objectives

This module will enable learners to

- Understand the steps of the collaborative negotiation process
- Explore negotiation skills
- Understand the mediation process
- Explore mediation skills
- Understand the consensus-building process
- Explore consensus-building skills
- Examine and apply negotiation, mediation, and consensus-building processes in the context of the educational environment
- Understand the impact of culture and power on conflict and conflict resolution processes

Background

Alternative dispute resolution (or conflict resolution, as it is often called) refers to a range of approaches: negotiation, conciliation, mediation, fact-finding, and arbitration. Among these various approaches, negotiation is the only approach that does not require a third party. Arbitration is the only approach that removes the final resolution from the hands of the disputants. Overall, these approaches can be defined and differentiated by

- The role of third parties
- The extent to which communication among the parties is formally structured
- The role of the disputing parties in shaping the final resolution
- The interests served through the resolution

Girard, Rifkin, and Townley (1985, pp. 1–2) summarized the basic approaches to conflict resolution as follows:

- *Negotiation.* Voluntary problem solving and/or bargaining carried out directly between the disputing parties in order to reach a joint agreement on common concerns
- *Conciliation.* Voluntary negotiation with the help of a third party who serves to bring the parties together to talk or who carries information between the parties
- *Mediation.* Voluntary participation in a structured process in

which a neutral third party helps disputants identify and satisfy their interests relative to their dispute

- *Fact-finding.* Investigation conducted by a neutral third party which results in a recommended settlement.
- *Arbitration.* Voluntary or required participation in a process of explaining, presenting, and justifying needs, interests, and/or positions which results in a binding or advisory settlement determined by a neutral third party.

As these definitions suggest, in negotiations only the interests of the individuals directly involved are considered. There is no third party. By contrast, the fact-finder (often an ombudsperson on college and university campuses) has a specific role, which may include ensuring that the policies, procedures, rules, and regulations of some larger body (such as a government, corporation, or educational institution) are fair in their conception and in their application. Fact-finders may recommend remedies beyond the individual case.

While mediation may seem similar to conciliation or assisted problem solving, it differs in some important ways. While conciliation is usually an informal process, emerging from the social or organizational context of the dispute and carried out between people who know one another, mediation is a formally structured process that must be specifically sought out and is guided by mediators who may be strangers to the disputants. Negotiation and conciliation depend upon the goodwill of all involved. Mediation does too, but to a large extent its success depends on the fairness of a highly structured process.

Collaborative Negotiation

Negotiation is a problem-solving process wherein two or more people voluntarily discuss their differences and attempt to reach a joint decision on their common concerns. Negotiation occurs among friends, among family members, and within and between organizations. In the educational setting, negotiations take place between teachers and students, between administrators and professors, between different departments, and between schools and parents.

Negotiation requires participants to identify points where they differ, teach each other about their respective needs and interests, create various possible solutions, and reach agreement about what will be done. Negotiating is the principal way that old relationships are redefined and new relationships created.

Negotiating is a step-by-step process that places communication and thinking skills into a framework that guides the participants toward discovering a mutually satisfactory agreement. Since negotiation is an unassisted process—that is, a process that does not involve a third party—participants guide themselves through the process of expressing what they need, testing the receptivity and issues of the other party or parties, and attempting to obtain the most satisfactory solution.

According to Moore (1986), a number of preconditions make success in negotiations more likely. Although they are not absolutely necessary prerequisites for negotiating, these conditions can affect the final outcome. Negotiations are more likely to be successful when

1. The people involved in the conflict can be identified and are willing to "sit down at the bargaining table" to discuss the problem.

2. The participants are interdependent—that is, they need each other in some way to have their needs or interests satisfied.

3. The participants can agree upon some common issues and interests.

4. There is some sense of urgency or a deadline.

5. At least some part of the issue is negotiable.

6. The people involved want to settle the dispute more than they want to continue it.

7. There are no major psychological barriers to settlement.

8. The individuals involved have the authority to make a decision.

9. External factors (views of others, political climate, public opinion, economic conditions) are favorable to settlement.

10. The participants have the resources (communication skills, thinking skills, time) to negotiate [adapted from Moore, 1986, p. 11].

Bodine, Crawford, and Schrumpf (1994) note that the skillful negotiator strives to be an empathic listener, suspends judgment, is respectful, and has a cooperative spirit. Negotiation works best when the disputants view themselves as partners trying to solve a problem, not as individuals on opposing sides.

The collaborative negotiation process involves six steps:

1. Agree to negotiate.

2. Gather points of view.

3. Find common interests.

4. Create win-win options.

5. Evaluate options.

6. Create an agreement.

By *agreeing to negotiate*, participants indicate their willingness to work together toward a solution, as well as their interest in hearing one another's point of view. Depending upon the age and maturity of the parties and the nature and history of the dispute, ground rules (an agreement to take turns talking, to be honest, to focus directly on the problem) may need to be stated at the outset.

Gathering points of view is the education stage of a negotiation. While one disputant explains his or her view of the problem, the other uses the active listening techniques of nonverbal attending, asking clarifying questions, and summarizing both facts and feelings.

This is the stage where identifying one another's underlying needs and interests is important. Consider the classic conflict resolution case posed by Mary Parker Follett (Hocker and Wilmot, 1991, p. 214): Two men are quarreling in the library. One wants the window open; the other wants the window closed. (Those are the positions.) The two argue about how much to leave the window open, with no solution arising that satisfies them both. Finally, the librarian arrives and asks the one why he wants the window open. "To get some fresh air," he replies. She asks the other why he wants the window closed. He replies, "To avoid the draft." (These are the needs or interests.) The question then becomes how they can bring in fresh air but avoid a draft. The solution is to open a window in the next room.

During the stage where points of view are expressed, a useful activity for the listener is to put himself or herself in the other person's shoes. Asking yourself why the other holds a particular view and asking the other to explain why he or she takes a particular position are useful for increasing and clarifying understanding of the real problem.

Step three, *finding common interests*, is the crucial point in the negotiation process. According to Fisher, Ury, and Patton (1991), there are three significant points about shared interests that the negotiator needs to keep in mind:

1. Shared interests lie latent in every negotiation, although they may not be immediately obvious. A shared interest might be as simple as a mutual desire to preserve a relationship or a shared need to avoid the consequences of a failure to reach resolution.

2. Shared interests are opportunities, but for them to be of use, you must make something of them. A shared interest needs to be explicit and stated as a shared goal.

3. Stressing shared interests can make a negotiation smoother and more pleasant for all concerned. Once participants in a dispute are focused upon their shared interests, they will be willing to subordinate some individual differences [adapted from Fisher, Ury, and Patton (1991), p. 73].

Finding common interests entails exchanging information about what you need and why you need it, as well as listening to one another and summarizing what the other side needs and why. Finding common interests requires respectful probing behind the immediate positions in a search for points of agreement.

Finding common interests gives the disputants hope, which greatly increases the success potential of the next step in the negotiation process—*creating win-win options.* This is where creative brainstorming is best utilized. Thinking of possible solutions— options for mutual gain—is the joint responsibility of all parties to the dispute.

This is not the time for looking for the single best answer; rather, it is a time for generating a large number of potential answers, working together. Criticizing too soon or deciding on a particular course of action prematurely are risks to be avoided at this stage.

Step five, *evaluating options,* is the point in the negotiation process where participants look at their list of possibilities and consider what they think will work, what is best for all, and what each is willing to do. Asking questions like "What do you think would be a fair agreement?"—disregarding for the moment who will do what—is often a useful way to begin evaluating possible choices. Fisher and Ury (1981) suggest that agreements need to be based on objective standards that both sides accept. Such standards may be based on efficiency, precedent, community practices, equal treatment, scientific merit, or other measures. In the absence of objective standards, a fair procedure for deriving terms may be effective in helping the disputants decide together what action will be taken.

The final step in collaborative negotiation is *formalizing the agreement.* This might be as simple as each side telling the other what they will do. The agreement might also be a jointly written memorandum of understanding or a contract. In the final step, implementation details like who, what, when, where, and how need to be stated clearly to avoid misunderstanding. It is also a good idea for the participants to agree on a time in the near future to check in with one another to be sure the resolution is working satisfactorily for all concerned. (Exhibit 3.2 provides a detailed outline of the collaborative negotiation process.)

Negotiation depends upon the communication behavior of the participants. Cultural factors, including ethnicity, gender, and other personal characteristics, affect communication behaviors, and therefore they have considerable impact on the negotiating process and the potential outcomes of a negotiation. Men often communicate differently from women. An African American may communicate differently from a European American. Both may communicate differently from a Native American. Assumptions about others based on their gender or ethnicity can affect the negotiation process. The more understanding a participant has of cultural, ethnic, and gender differences, the more likely the negotiation process will proceed with respect for all concerned.

Power is also a constant presence and influence in any conflict situation. According to Hocker and Wilmot (1991), power may flow from expertise, control of resources, interpersonal connections, or communication skills. Institutionalized policies, rules, and practices (along with informal controls) give members of one group more power than others. In the United States, men, Caucasians, heterosexuals, middle-aged persons, able-bodied persons, members of the middle or upper class, and Christians have accrued or had access to greater power. At the same time, power differences among members of these groups are substantial. Language, education, health, appearance, and marital status are also power variables. If one party in a negotiation has more power than the other (or is perceived to have more), the conflict is unbalanced. Balancing the participants' power through the use of restraint, empowerment, or transcendence is often a significant factor in successfully negotiating an agreement. If power imbalances cannot be successfully addressed, a third party may be necessary. (See Appendix D, "Exploring the Dynamics of Power in Conflict Resolution," for more information on the subject.)

The first choice for resolving conflict is negotiation, because when it is engaged in correctly by skillful negotiators, it allows the parties in a dispute complete freedom to solve their problem together. This experience is highly satisfying and builds a sense of self-control and self-esteem. If the negotiation doesn't work out, the next logical step is to seek assistance from a third party, a mediator.

Mediation

Mediation is an extension of the negotiation process. However, while negotiation may be either very formal, as in contract negotiations, or very informal, as in friends negotiating differing needs for dinner, mediation refers to a formal, albeit collaborative, process. While mediation programs and mediators differ somewhat in their approach, most use some combination of the following components:

- *An intake session.* In this session the disputing parties are told about mediation and interviewed about the nature of the conflict. A decision is then made by each party, working with a third party, as to whether or not the conflict should be mediated.

- *Selection of a mediator or mediator team.* This process is based primarily on the need to facilitate the disputing parties' trust in the mediator or mediators.

- *Joint sessions.* In these sessions, disputants provide information on the issues at the heart of the dispute and on their needs, concerns, positions, and interests, in the presence of the other party and the mediator or mediator team.

- *Individual sessions.* In these sessions, disputants meet privately with the mediator or mediators to go over their concerns, interests, and needs in more detail, without the presence of the other party.

- *Mediator caucuses.* At this point, the mediator or mediators take time apart from the disputants to devise a strategy for the next session.

- *An agreement.* Once an agreement is reached, the mediator or mediator team writes (most typically) or verbally summarizes the agreement reached by the disputing parties.

One can see that mediation relies upon basically the same processes as collaborative negotiation. The difference is that the steps of gathering points of view, finding common interests, creating win-win options, and evaluating options are guided by the mediator within the structured framework of joint and individual sessions.

Not all conflicts can be mediated, and some issues may not be appropriate to mediation at all. Should sexual harassment be mediated, for example? Some practitioners in the field say never. Others think that it depends on the specifics of the case and the parties. While divorce often entails a complex set of conflicting feelings, needs, concerns, positions, and interests, divorce can be successfully mediated. Typically, mediated divorces take half the time and are viewed as more satisfactory than those conducted in an adversarial way. In schools, offenses involving weapons and physical injury are usually deemed inappropriate for mediation, while infractions of other rules are referred to mediation instead of traditional disciplinary channels. School mediation programs utilizing peer mediators report resolution rates of up to 95 percent (Schrumpf, Crawford, & Usadel, 1991).

In general, mediation may be the best choice when the conflict is a long-standing one, when past efforts to negotiate have failed, when one disputant feels the other is more powerful or can't be trusted, or when those who might act as informal conciliators or problem solvers have roles or vested interests related to the dispute. In all cases, mediation, like negotiation or conciliation, must be voluntary on all sides.

The role of the mediator is to "facilitate the parties to the dispute to reach an agreement themselves" (Keltner, quoted in Hocker & Wilmot, 1991). The mediator who can encourage and facilitate creative thinking among disputants often has the best chance for reaching a successful resolution (Koch & Decker, 1993). Identifying who will be the most appropriate and effective mediator for a given dispute is not an easy task. Trust in the mediator is essential. For this reason, many mediation programs attempt to match mediator and disputant characteristics. Programs may also use teams of mediators to increase the possibility of matching factors such as age, race, ethnicity, and gender. A team can also help to decrease the probability of a sole mediator's being seen as allied with only one party. Teams also increase the mediators' ability to keep track of needs, issues, and options.

Another aspect of mediator selection has to do with professional standards in the field. Mediators learn their skills in a variety of ways—through formal university programs, workshops, practical experience, and supervision. Mediators are often, but not always, professionals in fields that extensively utilize mediation processes, such as the law, counseling, and social work. There are numerous certification programs for mediators, although standards and requirements vary widely. In general, education, experience, involvement in professional mediation organizations, adherence to standards of ethical conduct, and personal and professional reputation are indicators of a mediator's qualification.

Mediation usually begins with the mediators' introducing themselves and explaining the process. The issue of confidentiality is always addressed. It is often appropriate to agree to discuss only the agreement, as opposed to the issues underlying the conflict, outside of the mediation event. Additionally, depending on the age of the parties involved, ground rules such as listening attentively, not interrupting, and being cooperative may be discussed. In general, the mediator or mediators attempt to set a tone for the session and to indicate that they will be directing the process.

Mediation involves guiding and managing the steps defined above for collaborative negotiation: gather points of view, find common interests, create win-win options, and evaluate options. In mediation these steps are achieved either through joint sessions or through a combination of joint, individual, and caucus sessions.

Some mediators never use individual sessions; others use them frequently. Some mediators use caucuses frequently; others use them rarely or never. Exercise 3.5 provides more detailed descriptions of each session type.

Whether only joint sessions or both joint and individual sessions are used, the mediator or mediators supervise and structure the exchange of information, guide discussion, ask open-ended questions, and help the participants understand the concepts of BATNA and WATNA. (See the Glossary. These are terms coined by Fisher and Ury in *Getting to Yes*, 1981.) The mediator or mediators seek to ensure that each participant has equal opportunity to participate and that each fully understands the other's point of view.

The final step of mediation, like the final step of negotiation, is to create an agreement. This step can be as unsophisticated as asking each party to state what they have agreed to or as formal as drawing up a written document signed by all parties, including the mediators.

Although no conflict resolution process guarantees specific outcomes, there are several benefits to mediation. Mediation is less expensive than litigation. Mediation usually facilitates rapid settlements. Mediation can address power imbalances by having a third party structure the exchange of information. Participants in mediation are usually satisfied with the process and the results. Finally, there is a high rate of compliance when a mediator is used (Moore, 1986).

The use of mediation has been growing in the education field. Colleges and universities have found that mediation offers an alternative to formal legal proceedings. Campuses have used mediation to handle roommate conflicts and tenant-landlord disputes. Others have created mediation services encompassing the full range of conflicts experienced by people living and working together. Still others have incorporated mediation into grievance procedures (Girard, Rifkin, & Townley, 1985).

As part of this movement, interdisciplinary conflict resolution certificate programs have developed, as have graduate degree programs. Trained mediators from colleges and universities are working with teachers and students in elementary, middle, and high schools to support the development of mediation in all educational settings. Mediation offers educators a model for promoting people's abilities to make decisions about their lives, for fostering respect and cooperation, and for developing the use of fairness rather than power in decision making. These are goals shared by educators at many levels of our education system. Fortunately, by the very nature of their commitment to human development, many educators already possess the basic communication and organization skills necessary to act as problem solvers for their colleagues and students. These skills easily become a foundation for involvement in more formal mediation.

Consensus Building

Consensus building is a helpful tool for applying conflict resolution techniques in group settings. When a conflict affects many or all members of a group (for example, faculty in a college of education or students in a class), consensus building provides a framework for building an integrative solution that uses creative contributions from all members of the group to satisfy as many interests as possible. Following steps similar to the negotiation and mediation models, consensus building results in an agreement to which everyone can subscribe—although everyone may not like the solution equally well (Koch & Decker, 1993). The consensus decision-making model can be valuable because the information flow and range of options explored may be greater than when subgroups are delegated to make decisions or when voting is used.

Obviously, facilitating the consensus-building process requires communication skills, sensitivity, and careful organization. Like the mediator in a mediation, the facilitator in a consensus-building session is the expert on the process, responsible for designing and implementing an effective procedure that enables participants to focus on the substantive issues under discussion. Facilitating consensus building is similar to holding the baton above an orchestra. In order to make music, careful coordination is required.

The facilitator's job is to encourage the presentation of diverse viewpoints in ways that encourage all group members to speak and to listen for points of agreement as well as areas where opinions differ. The steps for consensus building, although slightly more complex due to the increased number of participants, are a reflection of the progression from gathering information to creating solutions and agreements. (Exhibit 3.6 provides a detailed breakdown of the consensus-building process.)

Although according to most dictionaries *consensus* means unanimity, in conflict resolution practice it does not. It does mean that an agreement is the best one, in the eyes of the group, for the group as a whole. It reflects a considered agreement that everyone involved—unanimously—accepts a specific course of action as best for the group and agrees to support it regardless of private preferences and interests. Consensus encourages a deeper level of conflict analysis and encourages all participants in the negotiation to express their opinions and concerns.

Successful consensus building and the resolutions that result from the process are far more dependent upon the activity of the third party—the facilitator—than other conflict resolution processes. For this reason, a skillful and experienced facilitator is essential to the process.

References

Bodine, R. J., Crawford, D., & Schrumpf, F. (1994). *Creating the peaceable school.* Champaign, IL: Research Press.

Fisher, R., & Ury, W. (1981). *Getting to yes: Negotiating agreement without giving in.* Boston: Houghton Mifflin.

Fisher, R., Ury, W., and Patton, B. (1991). *Getting to yes: Negotiating agreement without giving in (second edition).* New York: Penguin Books.

Girard, K., Rifkin, J., & Townley, A. (1985). *Peaceful persuasion: A guide to creating mediation dispute resolution programs on college campuses.* Washington, DC: National Institute for Dispute Resolution.

Hocker, J., & Wilmot, W. (1991). *Interpersonal conflict* (3rd ed.). Dubuque, IA: W. C. Brown.

Koch, S., & Decker, R. (1993). "Applying conflict resolution techniques in school negotiations." *School Business Affairs, 59*(8), 17–20.

Moore, C. (1986). *The mediation process: Practical strategies for resolving conflict.* San Francisco: Jossey-Bass.

Schrumpf, F., Crawford, D., & Usadel, H. C. (1991). *Peer mediation: Conflict resolution in schools.* Champaign, IL: Research Press.

Exercises

Conflict resolution processes are best understood through first-hand experience with an actual conflict. The following exercises attempt to simulate such experience. Skill development for negotiation, mediation, and consensus building requires analysis, practice, and processing.

 ## Exercise 3.1. Beautiful Butterfly Case Revisited

NOTE: This exercise deals with the same situation as Exercise 1.5. It should be used in one module or the other—not both. In this module, the goal of the exercise is to identify a key skill in negotiating: separating positions from interests. The point of this exercise here is to allow you—and the participants themselves—to see how members of your class intuitively approach the problem. You should just let them go to it—do not give them specific negotiation guidelines before they start.

Objectives

- Develop understanding of the collaborative negotiation process
- Enhance negotiation skills

Procedures

1. Instruct the participants to find a partner with whom they have not yet worked. Give each partner an exhibit for either Dr. Hirera (Exhibit 1.2[b]) or Dr. James (Exhibit 1.2[a]), and advise them not to look at each other's scripts.

2. Direct the participants to read their respective role assignments privately and then negotiate a settlement with their simulation partner. Remind them that each doctor's job depends on the results of the deal.

3. Allow about fifteen minutes, then reassemble the group and ask each pair how they solved the problem. Usually at least one has figured out that Dr. James needs the cocoons and Dr. Hirera needs the adult butterflies. Explore how they came to this discovery, pointing out the difference between needs and interests.

4. Summarize the purpose of the activity and ask for reactions.

Exercise 3.2. Power Shuffle

NOTE: The parties to any conflict differ from one another in both fundamental and minor ways. Regardless of similarities, there are always cultural differences present that affect the outcome of the encounter. Additionally, power is a constant presence and influence in any conflict situation. This exercise will help participants identify and acknowledge various groups and explore power differences between and among individuals and groups.

Objective

- Understand the impact of culture and power on conflict and conflict resolution processes

Procedures

1. Ask participants to gather at one end of the room.

2. Explain that you are going to give a series of instructions related to group affiliation and that the participants should follow these instructions silently. After each one, they should look around, paying attention to who is with them and who is separated from them—and to the way they feel at each stage of the exercise.

Reassure the group that participation is purely voluntary, and they do not need to identify themselves as members of any group if they do not wish to. Point out that anyone uncertain about their membership in a given group should simply make a quick, personal choice about where it makes sense to go. In addition, note that for most people of color, there is not a choice in this.

3. Go through the list of affinity statements in Exhibit 3.1. For each group, ask people who regard themselves as members of that group to move across the room from the class, turn, and look back. Have the two groups stand still for a moment, observing each other and their own feelings. Then bring them together again for the next shuffle.

Here is a script for the exercise: "Please step to the other side of the room if you are [category]. (Pause). Notice who is standing with you and who is not. (Pause). Notice how you feel. (Pause). Come back together."

4. At the end of the list, ask all participants to walk to the center of the room and, for a few minutes, mingle silently, making eye contact and acknowledging one another as people present together in this group.

5. Get the group seated, then go over the exercise. Use the following process questions to enrich the discussion:

    a. What feelings emerged when you were engaged in this exercise? When? Why?

    b. What did you like about this exercise?

    c. What did you dislike about this exercise?

    d. What identified groups would you say had more power? Why?

    e. What identified groups would you say had less power? Why?

    f. What did you learn from participating in this exercise?

    g. What does this exercise have to do with conflict and conflict resolution processes?

Note: Instructors might want to raise the following for discussion:

- Feelings of powerfulness and powerlessness affect anger and despair, which are important components of conflict and conflict resolution.

- Societal bias affects powerfulness and powerlessness.

- Group membership has an impact on problem solving and perceptions of fairness of the conflict resolution process.

Exhibit 3.1.   Group Affinity List

Please step to the other side of the room if

a. You are a woman.
b. You are African American, or black, or of African descent.
c. You are Latino, Chicano, or mestizo.
d. You are Asian, East Indian, Indian, or Pacific Islander.
e. You are of Arabian descent.
f. You are Native American, or at least one of your parents or grandparents is full-blooded Native American.
g. You are of Jewish heritage.
h. You are over 45.
i. You were raised poor.
j. You are currently a single parent.
k. You were raised in a working class family where most people did manual labor or pink-collar work to make a living.
l. You were raised in an isolated community.
m. You were raised Catholic.
n. You have a visible or hidden physical disability or impairment.
o. You have ever been dangerously or continuously sick or near death.
p. Your native language is other than English.
q. You come from a family where alcohol or other drugs was a problem.
r. You are lesbian, gay, or bisexual or have friends who are lesbian, gay, or bisexual. *Note:* Since the civil rights and safety of homosexuals are not guaranteed in the United States, this item includes the statement "or have friends who are lesbian, gay, or bisexual" to allow people to indicate affinity without declaring membership in this minority group. Do not remove the qualifying statement!
s. You have a family member who is HIV positive or has AIDS.
t. You or a member of your family has ever been labeled mentally ill.
u. You have ever been publicly labeled fat.
v. You have ever been unemployed, not by choice.
w. You do not have tenure in your faculty position.
x. You have ever been a child.

Note: This exercise is based heavily on one presented by Harrison Simms in *Helping Teens Stop Violence* and is used here with permission. (Creighton, A., & Kivel, P. [1992]. *Helping teens stop violence.* Alameda, CA: Hunter House.) The book is available though Hunter House Publishers, 1-800-266-5592; P. O. Box 2914, Alameda, CA, 94501, ordering @hunterhouse.com.

Exercise 3.3. Negotiation Simulation

NOTE: Experience in negotiation is crucial, as no amount of reading will generate the skill and adaptability needed to cope with the shifting demands of a dispute. Fortunately, most people find it possible to learn a great deal from arbitrary situations and need not wait to be personally involved. (*Note:* See Appendix B for role-play guidelines and Appendix C for some sample role-play scenarios.)

Objectives

- Develop understanding of the collaborative negotiation process
- Enhance negotiation skills
- Examine and apply the negotiation process in the context of the education environment

Procedures

1. Ask participants to assemble in groups of three. Have each group select one of their number to serve as observer while the other two act as disputants.

2. Give each group a copy of Exhibit 3.2, "Collaborative Negotiation Process," and give each disputant a set of information on one side of a hypothetical dispute. You can use the sample situations in Appendix C for this purpose, or you can develop new ones of your own. All the groups should work from the same situation.

3. Allow about five minutes for the participants to read their instructions, which should include a summary of the situation under dispute as known to both parties, the position being taken by the character assumed by the participant, and background information unique to that character.

4. Direct the disputants to negotiate, applying both the framework in Exhibit 3.2 and the communications and thinking skills discussed in earlier modules. Tell participants to feel free to stop briefly and consult with you as needed. Instruct the observer to take notes on the proceedings, noting actions that move the negotiation forward as well as actions that seem to inhibit the process.

5. Allow about twenty to thirty minutes for the negotiation. Then reassemble the group. Ask each triad to report their progress, from the point of view of the disputants and also as noted by the observer. Use the following process questions to enrich the discussion:

a. What went well?

b. What did not go well?

    c. What was most difficult?

    d. What would you do differently if you were to try again?

    e. What questions helped you get beyond positions to needs and interests?

    f. What is your solution?

    g. What did you learn from this experience?

    h. What did you like about this exercise?

    i. What did you dislike about this exercise?

Exhibit 3.2.   Collaborative Negotiation Process

1. Agree to negotiate.
   a. Express an interest and willingness to discuss the problem.
   b. Set a time and place to talk.
   c. Establish and agree on ground rules. (Depending on the situation, you may need to agree to take turns talking, to be honest, to focus directly on the problem, to avoid blaming and name-calling, and to agree on confidentiality.)
2. Gather points of view.
   a. Agree on who will talk first.
   b. Take turns stating the problem using "I" statements and clear descriptions. While one speaks, the other listens carefully and actively, asks open-ended questions, and conveys interest with nonverbal as well as verbal signals.
   c. Identify each other's needs and interests, separating positions from interests.
   d. Focus on the problem, the present, and the future.
   e. Reframe the problem in neutral terms.
3. Find common interests.
   a. Discuss and identify possible shared interests.
   b. Look for areas of agreement.
   c. State shared interests as a shared goal.
4. Create win-win options.
   a. Ask each person what a successful solution must include.
   b. Brainstorm possible solutions without evaluating them.
   c. Generate as many ideas as possible, stating the creative and unusual as well as the obvious.
5. Evaluate options.
   a. Review all ideas and options in terms of what each person needs.
   b. Discuss what is likely to work and what is probably not workable.
   c. Elaborate or improve ideas generated in step 4.
   d. Discuss probable outcomes or consequences of preferred options.
   e. Establish trade-offs, if trade-offs will be part of the agreement.
   f. Decide what each will do.
6. Create an agreement
   a. Develop a contract, written or oral.
   b. Establish a time and framework for checking back to see how the agreement is working.

 ### Exercise 3.4. Informal Mediation

NOTE: Successful mediation requires even more skill than negotiation. This skill can also be acquired in simulations, but it is very useful to be able to work with people who are already adept at the craft. If possible, invite several skilled mediators to serve as facilitators during the class session in which you introduce this exercise. (*Note:* See Appendix B for role-play guidelines and Appendix C for some sample role-play scenarios.)

Objectives

- Develop an understanding of the mediation process
- Enhance mediation skills
- Examine and apply the mediation process in the context of the education environment

Procedures

1. Assemble the full class and discuss the mediation process and the mediator's role, based on material in the Background section. Introduce the facilitators, if any (it is important to obtain outside help if the instructor is not experienced in the field of negotiation and mediation), at the beginning of this discussion, and make use of whatever additional information and insight they can provide. Make sure the discussion covers these issues:

    a. When is a mediator useful?

    b. Who should/should not mediate [type of dispute] in the education environment? Can the supervisor be a mediator?

    c. What is the difference between formal and informal mediation?

    d. What is the mediator's role in each?

    e. What is the difference between conciliation mediation and conciliation arbitration?

    f. What are special mediator-selection concerns in an intercultural dispute?

    g. When should mediation be used?

2. Explain that this exercise will be an informal mediation experience. Using Exhibit 3.2, "Collaborative Negotiation Process," participant-mediators will help two disputants negotiate a dispute,

using communication, brainstorming, and other techniques as they appear applicable. Point out that the participants chosen as mediators should initiate the process by stating something like, "I understand that there is a problem and that you both think I may be able to help you to examine it together so that you can get it resolved. Is that right?" The disputants should promptly agree—it is far too early in the learning process to experiment with refusal to talk.

3. Have participants assemble in groups of three and select one of their number to serve as mediator for a dispute involving the other two. Make sure each group has a copy of Exhibit 3.2 on hand.

4. Distribute role assignments to the two disputants. You can use the sample situations in Appendix C for this purpose, or you can develop new ones of your own. All the groups should work from the same situation.

5. Allow about five minutes for the participants to read their instructions, which should include a summary of the situation under dispute (as it is understood by both parties), the position being taken by the character assumed by the participant, and background information unique to that character.

6. Direct the mediators to get started. While the participants work on the problem, try to tune in on the process in each group, and provide over-the-shoulder coaching as needed. If you have facilitators available, ask them to coach as needed—this is where they will prove most useful.

7. Allow about twenty minutes, then reassemble the group and ask each triad to report their progress. Use the following process questions to enrich the discussion:

    a. What went well?

    b. What did not go well?

    c. What was the most difficult issue for the mediator? for the disputants?

    d. What would you do differently if you were to try again?

    e. What questions helped you get beyond positions to needs and interests?

    f. What is your solution?

    g. What did you learn from this experience?

    h. What did you like about this exercise?

    i. What did you dislike about this exercise?

    j. Would a more formal process have been a help? a hindrance?

Exercise 3.5. Formal Mediation Demonstration

NOTE: This exercise is designed to allow participants to observe a professional mediator in action. It also introduces the concept of comediation. Professional mediators are available in most communities, either through a local community mediation center, a college campus, or a bar association. Readers should contact NAME at NIDR for assistance in locating a mediator to serve as an outside resource. Another option is to select a video to illustrate a mediation. NAME can provide instructors with a list of available videos. We have used the Intercultural Case Study (see Appendix C) as the basis for a negotiation demonstration and a mediation demonstration because of the relevance of the issues raised in schools and on campuses nationally.

Objectives

- Develop an understanding of the mediation process
- Enhance mediation skills
- Examine and apply the mediation process in the context of the education environment

Procedures

1. Distribute copies of Exhibit 3.4, "Stages of the Mediation Process," to all participants.

2. Introduce the simulation by providing a brief description of the situation, the players and their position, and some background information. Have the mediator conduct a full mediation, including an initial joint session with the participants, a caucus, individual sessions, and a final joint session. Remember that this is a demonstration and that the participants—as well as the mediators—should be experienced people. The students serve as observers for the demonstration and can use questions a through i below or Exhibit 3.3.

3. After the mediation is complete, go over the exercise with the group. Use the following process questions to enrich the discussion:

    a. What went well?

    b. What did not go well?

    c. What seemed difficult?

    d. What seemed to be the benefits of using comediators?

e. What questions helped the participants get beyond positions to needs and interests?

f. What did you learn about the problem that you didn't know before?

g. What did you think was crucial information or an "ah-ha!" moment in this session?

h. What do you think about the progress so far or the solution?

i. Why was mediation more helpful than negotiation in this case?

Exhibit 3.3.   Questions for Observing the Mediation Demonstration

1. Can you identify three things the mediators did that demonstrated that they were active listeners?

   _____

   _____

2. What were the kinds of questions that elicited the most information from the disputants? Give an example.

   _____

   _____

3. Were there any techniques the mediators used that helped to de-escalate the situation? Give an example.

   _____

   _____

4. Describe the process that was used to generate creative solutions.

   _____

   _____

Exhibit 3.4.   Stages of the Mediation Process
_____

In this discussion, "you" refers to the mediator.
  1. Joint Session: Setting the Stage, Building Trust, and Fact-Finding
      a. Briefly introduce your role and the process to be used.
      b. Address the issue of confidentiality.
      c. Set the ground rules. (This may include agreeing to focus on the problem, deal honestly, and avoid blaming, name-calling, and interrupting.)
      d. Get a general picture of the problem by asking each participant to describe the situation as he or she sees it.
      e. Allow each person to hear the other's list of wants (positions).
  2. Caucus: Taking Time with Self or Comediator (*Note:* Hold a caucus after each meeting with any or all of the disputants.)
      a. Review notes: what do you know about the conflict? What do you still need to know about the conflict?
      b. Plan strategy: who to see first, what issues to deal with and in what order, what questions to ask.
      c. Anticipate possible difficulties with information you might get or might need to release, and plan how to selectively release positive information.
      d. In the final caucus, prepare a draft of the agreement. (Use the participants' language, and make sure the elements are balanced, specific, and clear.)
  3. Individual Sessions: Discovering Areas of Agreement
      a. Give each person a chance to speak without the pressure of the other's presence.
      b. Get the details of the situation.
      c. Determine the true interests.
      d. Identify areas of agreement.
      e. Generate and develop options.
      f. Use hypothetical situations to test possible solutions.
      g. Explore and get concessions if you believe they may be necessary.
      h. Get agreement for what each is willing to do.
  4. Joint Session: Reaching Agreement and Coming to Closure
      a. State identified shared interests and areas of agreement.
      b. Describe proposed solution elements from Step 3h. (Elements should be balanced, specific, and clear to both participants.)
      c. Review the agreement.
      d. State what each will do.
      e. Establish a way to follow up to see how the agreement is working.
_____

Exercise 3.6. Mediation Simulation

NOTE: This exercise enables participants to practice the comediator role. As with Exercise 3.4, it would be very useful for participants to be able to work with people who are already adept at the craft. If possible, invite several skilled mediators to serve as coaches during the class session in which you introduce this exercise. Setting up mediation role plays requires training and experience. Readers are advised not to attempt role playing without this training or the assistance of an experienced mediator. The structure used depends largely on the size of the group, but small groups of no more than nine are recommended, with two comediators, two disputants, up to four observers, and a professional mediator acting as a coach. (*Note:* See Appendix B for role-play guidelines and Appendix C for some sample role-play scenarios.)

Objectives

- Develop an understanding of the mediation process
- Enhance mediation skills
- Examine and apply the mediation process in the context of the education environment

Procedures

1. Ask participants to assemble in groups of four. Aim for as much diversity as possible in terms of group affiliation (see Exhibit 3.1). Have each group pick two disputants and two mediators.

2. Hand out copies of Exhibits 3.3 and 3.4 to everyone, and give the disputants copies of their simulation roles and background material. You can use the sample situations in Appendix C for this purpose, or develop new ones of your own. All groups should work from the same situation.

3. Allow about ten minutes for the disputants to read their instructions, which should include a summary of the situation under dispute as known to both parties, the position being taken by the character assumed by the participant, and background information unique to that character. At the same time, have the comediators discuss how they intend to proceed, using the mediation outline as a guide. Comediators should decide how they want to arrange the physical environment (chairs, tables, and so on).

4. Direct the mediators to get started. While the participants work on the mediation, and if you do not have a professional

mediator as a coach, try to tune in on the process in each group, and provide over-the-shoulder coaching as needed.

5. Allow about forty minutes. First have small groups debrief among themselves. Then reassemble the group and ask each smaller group to report on their significant learnings. Use the following process questions to enrich the discussion:

- a. What went well?
- b. What did not go well?
- c. What seemed difficult?
- d. What questions helped the participants get beyond positions to needs and interests?
- e. What did you learn about the problem that you didn't know before?
- f. What did you think was crucial information or an "ah-ha!" moment in this session?
- g. What do you think about the progress so far or the solution?
- h. If you could start over, what would you do differently?
- i. What was your solution, if one was developed?

Exercise 3.7. Group Consensus Building

NOTE: The consensus-building process is an opportunity for group resolution. Like the mediator in a mediation, the facilitator in a consensus-building session is the process expert who designs and implements an effective procedure that enables the participants to focus on the substantive issues under discussion. This exercise provides observation and experience in consensus building.

Objectives

- Understand the consensus-building process
- Examine and apply negotiation, mediation, and consensus-building processes in the context of the education environment

Procedure

1. Lead the participants in a group discussion of the concept of consensus building, based on information from the Background section. Make sure the group covers the benefits and limitations of consensus building, the qualities of a good facilitator, and an overview of the process.

Exhibit 3.5.   Consensus-Building Steps

1. Define the positions around the conflict.
   a. What are the positions?
   b. What do people want?
2. Explore the reasons for all the positions.
   a. Ask why each participant took his or her position.
   b. Discuss the underlying needs and interests of all the positions.
   c. Identify shared needs and interests.
3. Brainstorm possible solutions to the problem.
   a. Suggest many ideas.
   b. Do not evaluate.
4. Evaluate the solutions with respect to the positions. Use a checklist grid to help discover solutions that meet the most interests. (A checklist grid is a simple way of evaluating alternatives against a set of criteria the group selects. The process described here is adapted from Schwarz, R. M. [1994]. *The skilled facilitator: Practical wisdom for developing effective groups.* San Francisco: Jossey-Bass.)
   a. Discuss and select approximately five criteria against which to evaluate the solutions that have been generated by brainstorming.
   b. Draw a grid (see matrix in Figure 3.1), listing the solutions down the row side and the criteria across the columns. (Make a separate column for each criterion.) Each individual in the group should be listed under each criterion so the individual's scores can be recorded by the facilitator.
   c. Have the facilitator ask the group to rank each solution on a scale, say 1 to 5, with 5 representing the highest score possible for any one axis of a criterion and a solution. Each individual's rank of each solution against each criterion is recorded, and the totals of the rankings are recorded at the end of each row.
   d. Although one should resist thinking that mathematical formulas can determine the final decisions of the group, the facilitator should survey the group to see if there is consensus about the highest-ranked solutions. This will likely result in a discussion that will lead to a final decision. If it does not, either a new process can be tried or the same process repeated, with refined thinking on how to define the criteria, and the solutions reconsidered using the same process.
5. Make an agreement that maximizes satisfaction for as many interests as possible.
   a. Continue discussion and modification of ideas until everyone feels able to subscribe to the agreement, even if everyone is not equally satisfied.

Figure 3.1. Matrix for Evaluating Alternative Solutions

Solutions	Criteria												
	Criterion 1 x (weight)				Criterion 2 x (weight)				Criterion 3 x (weight)				Solution scores
	Ann	Al	Jo	Lee	Ann	Al	Jo	Lee	Ann	Al	Jo	Lee	
Solution 1													
Solution 2													
Solution 3													
Solution 4													
Solution 5													

Source: Schwarz, R. M. (1994). The skilled facilitator: Practical wisdom for developing effective groups, p. 167. San Francisco: Jossey-Bass. Reprinted by permission.

Exhibit 3.6.   The Consensus-Building Process: Steps for Facilitators

1. Prepare for the meeting.
   a. Consult group members to determine the desired outcome and what success should look like.
   b. Prepare meeting agenda by collecting agenda items from group members.
   c. Determine the priority for each agenda item, and order items on the agenda.
2. Begin the meeting.
   a. Use a focus exercise to get everyone's attention.
   b. Review the agenda and agree to the meeting goals.
   c. Explain the consensus-building process.
3. Define the issues and set an agenda.
   a. Have one person present the first agenda item and the issues it raises.
   b. Ask for comments from others, additional related issues, or reframing of the issues.
4. Uncover hidden interests.
   a. Ask participants what elements must be present or interests satisfied for an agreement to be reached on the issue at hand.
   b. Seek agreement among group members that they will accept those elements as the criteria a solution must meet.
5. Generate options. Ask the parties to generate possible solutions or options that might satisfy their stated interests. Use brainstorming, open discussion, what others have done, private thinking, trial-and-error suggestions.
6. Assess options.
   a. Review interests, needs, and concerns.
   b. Discuss and evaluate proposed solutions, and identify preferred options. Have group members state "What I like about—"
7. Reach an agreement.
   a. Eliminate solutions that do not meet the criteria or are otherwise unacceptable.
   b. Combine options to arrive at a solution that meets all the participants' needs.
   c. Test for agreement by restating the proposed solution.
   d. If the group cannot agree, back off and go back to an earlier stage to rework the issues.
   e. Restate and reconfirm the agreement to a solution.
8. Implement the agreement.
   a. Review the agreement.
   b. Identify and reach agreement on the steps needed for implementation.
9. Monitor the agreement.
   a. Make sure all agreements, implementation steps, and monitoring procedures are in writing.
   b. Design a monitoring procedure.
10. Evaluate the meeting.
    a. Determine what went well.
    b. Identify what could be done to improve the consensus-building process.

Applications for Conflict Resolution in Education

The current interest in conflict resolution in schools and classrooms has many roots—the early principles of our schooling system, the reforms of progressive education, and a variety of contemporary social and educational trends. This module provides an overview of some of the key links between conflict resolution theory and practice and our public education system. These links are philosophical, practical, and strategic, and they include conflict resolution theory and practice as a component of education in a number of different areas, such as cooperative learning, multicultural education, and violence prevention. These links will be discussed later in this module.

This module also provides an overview of the options and issues affecting the application of conflict resolution techniques by teachers, counselors, school administrators, and faculty members responsible for teacher education programs. Emphasis is placed on the criteria to be considered in planning how to implement conflict resolution strategies. Three basic assumptions guide this module:

1. Conflict resolution in the schools is not a fad. Rather, it is a means of addressing core elements of every school and classroom.

2. The decision to include the study of conflict resolution techniques in teachers' professional preparation must be based on a clear rationale.

3. Because conflict resolution strategies are a relatively new innovation in education, it is essential that educators be well prepared to introduce them in the classroom and that

they be able to make effective decisions about how to do so. If conflict resolution theory and practice are to become an integral part of our system of education, they will do so through effective teacher training (both pre-service and in-service) and the advocacy of teachers, counselors, and administrators.

Objectives

This module enables learners to

- Explore the various ways in which conflict resolution theory and skills support fundamental goals of our educational system

- Explore the ways in which conflict resolution theory and skills address current issues and concerns in our public schools

- Develop a rationale for including conflict resolution in the schools

- Establish a personal vision for participants' place and work in the field

- Identify goals to be met by incorporating conflict resolution theory and practice into educators' professional lives

- Identify the best means to achieve these goals

- Identify practical criteria that will affect the goals and approach finally selected and implemented

- Identify potential barriers to implementing conflict resolution in professional activities, curricula, or instruction, and explore possible solutions

- Identify the development and implementation steps—including training, assistance, and approval by others—required to introduce and practice conflict resolution techniques in the schools

Background

The challenge to educators is to develop a broad understanding of the foundations of conflict resolution and then apply that understanding in the various contexts of the education discipline. That application may vary, depending upon program needs and structure and the individual practitioner's background and interests.

Conflict resolution programs in the schools first emerged in the early 1970s, sparked by the increasing concern of educators and parents about violence in the schools. The Children's Project for Friends, a Quaker program that teaches nonviolence in the New York City Schools, was the first to introduce conflict resolution ideas into U.S. schools. The Children's Creative Response to Conflict Program, which emerged from that effort, has since trained thousands of teachers.

With the establishment of Educators for Social Responsibility in 1981 and the National Association for Mediation in Education in 1984, the movement for conflict resolution in the schools became further organized. The purpose of NAME is to promote the development, implementation, and institutionalization of school- and university-based conflict resolution programs and curricula. As of the fall of 1995, NAME and NIDR estimated that there were over six thousand school-based conflict resolution programs operating in the United States and that over three hundred thousand students had been trained in basic collaborative negotiation techniques. In some school districts, conflict resolution education is mandated for all students, and a few states have legislative mandates related to the institution of conflict resolution programs in schools.

The spread of conflict resolution programs in U.S. schools reflects not only a recognition of the need to prevent school violence but also, at a more value-based level, an increased emphasis on empowerment and voluntarism. The idea that students can participate in and resolve their own conflicts and assume at least partial responsibility for their school's climate is a foundational principle of conflict resolution programs. From a long-range point of view, conflict resolution programs are meant to contribute to the development of individuals as self-governing and self-regulating members of school—and of society.

Conflict resolution programs in schools consist of several components: a student curriculum, peer mediation programs, leadership and staff development programs, parent and family initiatives, and changes in policies and procedures to establish a more cooperative school environment. Although schools do not always institute a comprehensive approach that includes all of those elements, conflict resolution programs have often grown from one element (such as a peer mediation program) to include developmentally appropriate curricula for all students and education and support for teachers, administrators, and other school staff.

In some schools, conflict resolution strategies are a part of the curricula for social studies, language arts, health education, and citizenship education. But with the increasing concern about violence in schools, conflict resolution is more and more often presented as an independent discipline, with its own curriculum and specialized activities.

This module discusses nine entry points for including conflict resolution programs in schools:

- Education for democracy
- Progressive education
- Cooperative learning
- Education in a multicultural society
- Multicultural education
- Constructive responses to patterns of injustice
- Violence prevention
- Critical thinking
- Site-based management

Education for Democracy

Modern democracy is founded on Rousseau's concepts linking citizen participation in lawmaking to moral responsibility and human dignity. According to his radical social contract, no law can be really legitimate unless it is an expression of the general will, a consensus of the whole community. Although the United States operates under a representative system of democracy, Rousseau's notion that each citizen has an obligation to participate in government remains a fundamental principle of our system of government—and our schools.

In the century following the Revolutionary War, the nation's educational policies flowed from its ideals of democracy, equality, and freedom. Since the viability of the republic depended upon the consent of the governed, everyone (definition subject to change) would have to be educated to meet their responsibilities as citizens. If the republic was to function as a united whole, then the people would need a common language and shared values related to citizenship. If achievements were to be judged based on talent, effort, and accomplishment rather than on social, economic, or national origin, then everyone would have to have an equal opportunity for education. Our public debate still centers on these ideals and appropriate ways of interpreting and meeting them.

Recent political and economic reform movements in central and eastern Europe and in the former Soviet Union have renewed interest in education for democracy. Various educational initiatives, including Partners for Democratic Change (which grew from the San Francisco Community Board Program) and the Orava Project (a University of Northern Iowa–Slovak Republic partnership), have introduced educational reform and conflict resolution programs in schools in the emerging democracies.

Conflict resolution, in its essence, is about engagement and productive participation. It is about expressing and resolving differences in order to achieve a mutual benefit. It is about ways of managing differences that cannot be easily (or ever) resolved. To participate in conflict resolution is to be willing to risk confronting differences of opinion and accepting alternative outcomes. Conflict resolution provides both the skills that support democratic participation and the experiences of productive conflict that build a cohesive social fabric. As processes that depend upon listening, negotiating, mediating, and cooperating rather than on power and position, they reflect democratic ideals.

Progressive Education

Although the curricula originally developed in the United States to meet these ideals fell short, emphasizing rigid structures, recitation, and memorized facts, the progressive ideas and practices that developed in the first part of this century strengthened the emphasis on social education. Many educators still respond to Dewey's charge (1949) to create "embryonic social communities" in schools to train children in community membership as a means of guaranteeing a fair and harmonious larger society. Conflict resolution curricula, law-related education curricula, and peacemaking curricula all advance the notion of the classroom as a community. One cannot teach any of these concepts effectively without applying them to the classroom environment. Each application strengthens student and teacher awareness of the class as a community and of that community as a learning experience of central importance.

Cooperative Learning

There is substantial evidence supporting the value of cooperative learning (Johnson & Johnson, 1989; Deutsch, 1991). Students who engage in cooperative learning activities develop commitment, helpfulness, and caring for one another despite differences in ability, gender, ethnicity, and so on. Cooperative learning also seems linked to higher self-esteem, positive attitudes toward school, and developing skills in taking new perspectives, acknowledging others' feelings, and collaborating. As summarized by Deutsch (1991), the elements of cooperative learning include acceptance of interdependence, substantial interaction time, individual accountability, interpersonal skills, group skills, and evaluation or analyzing skills. Deutsch also points out that cooperative learning provides a constructive social experience. Conflict resolution teaches skills that support a cooperative learning environment: interpersonal communication, accountability, and analysis.

Education in a Multicultural Society

Census data show that in the last thirty years, the United States has gained over twenty million new legal immigrants. Sixty-two percent of these immigrants came to the United States from Asian countries, Mexico, and Central America. Almost half of all those legally admitted to the United States in 1990 located in just five areas: Los Angeles, New York City, Chicago, Anaheim, and Houston. Recent immigration patterns, coupled with historical factors such as the forced relocation of African and Native American peoples and the appropriation of Spanish- and French-held territories, have created complex social problems in the United States for which there are no simple moral or pragmatic answers.

In some urban areas, signage solely in languages and alphabets other than English signals the boundaries of groups bound together by a minority culture and language. Often they are bound by a different economy as well. How do we prepare people for the potential problems and confusions of spontaneous "international" cross-cultural experiences in the United States? How do we turn differences in language and customs into a resource instead of a boundary? Is that an achievable goal?

Questions abound: Should every American speak English? To what country do people owe their allegiance? Do immigrants help or hurt the economy? These questions arise from living in a changing, diverse society, and they are actively confronted and argued every day. Multiculturalism, especially for those living in racially and ethnically diverse areas (such as population centers like New York City and Los Angeles that receive the highest numbers of new immigrants), is not an abstract concept pertaining to our history as a country but a concrete experience of daily life. Too often that experience is one of fear or frustration, of confusion and uncertain expectations on all sides.

In one Los Angeles school there are more than eighty primary languages. English is the third most common language in that school. Language barriers to communication are obvious. Behavioral barriers to good communication can be more subtle. Behaviors reflecting different cultural norms and values can result in gross misinterpretations of intention and meaning. Teachers used to think it was a challenge to recognize and address the needs of different levels of ability within the classroom. Teaching to "the middle," an abstract sense of the average child in the class, was, for many, a comforting possibility. In many classrooms there is now no illusion of an "average" child. What is the teacher's role in classrooms where children speak different primary languages, wrestle with their identity amid clashing cultures, and find that the curriculum doesn't reflect their experience?

Conflict resolution provides no answers to the dilemmas posed by our multicultural society, but it does offer skills and frameworks for handling differences, which can lead to improved communication, greater understanding, and less fear.

Multicultural Education

A truly multicultural curriculum goes far beyond the tourist approach to viewing other cultures. Instead, it looks at the ways we are similar and the ways we are different. It takes us into the realm of our fear of differences so that we can move beyond those fears, beyond prejudice, bias, and stereotype and into a positive understanding of "other." The themes of seeing, hearing, and speaking clearly are a part of both multicultural education and conflict resolution. The themes of recognizing when assumptions and stereotypes affect our attitudes and behaviors toward others are central to multicultural education and to conflict resolution. Awareness of one's own and others' culture and how it affects our norms, values, and behavior is important in multicultural education and in conflict resolution. Just as conflict resolution education offers practice in skills basic to the goals of multicultural education, so does multicultural education teach the awareness, knowledge, and values needed for effective conflict resolution.

Constructive Responses to Patterns of Injustice

Many analyses of violence in our society identify two key concepts: rage is a predictable response on the part of those who experience injustice, and hate crimes and harassment are manifestations of prejudice. Violence related to historical patterns of prejudice and injustice happens daily in our schools. When a context of injustice exists, whether it is related to age, gender, race, sexual orientation, ethnicity, physical ability, religion, or social class, small incidents become catalysts for large releases of anger. Small words, behaviors, slights, or provocations can stand, at any moment, for all the accumulated frustrations and resentments that have gone unaddressed over time. Often the sources of these frustrations and resentments are so deeply embedded in the fabric of daily life that they appear unchangeable.

Those who find themselves without power in a society with a pattern of discrimination and prejudice may experience a range of feelings related to their sense of powerlessness. These feelings may include fear, hopelessness, and despair as well as anger. In childhood and youth there is a general feeling of powerlessness that comes from being "only a kid" and the emotional turmoil of developing independence, peer acceptance, and identity. In this sense, most children feel themselves to be powerless and look for ways and opportunities to assert power. Prejudices learned from family, friends, and society at large can provide a seemingly easy means of gaining a sense of power and group identification. Prejudice, then, becomes a major flashpoint for interactions in schools.

Conflict resolution processes can play a part in providing both a communication framework and a constructive outlet for discussing the prejudice that underlies the feelings students bring to and derive from their experiences. Constructive communication experiences in school may provide some sense of power and thus prevent eruptions of violence. The same processes can serve as tools for interviewing the subjects of harassment and hate crimes, to increase the school community's understanding of what causes such crimes and find ways to decrease their occurrence. In this context, conflict resolution processes may be less about resolving disputes and more about creating channels for communication and understanding.

Violence Prevention

In many inner-city neighborhoods, children are exposed to violence on a daily basis. Yet even in suburban and rural communities, today's children run the risk of exposure to violence at home, in their neighborhoods, and in their schools. Especially for young children, the implicit contract between child and parent is that the adult will keep the child safe. What too many children now experience is a violation of that contract, directly through abuse at home or indirectly as they witness the failure of adults to keep violence at bay. Parents cannot stop bullets from being fired in the street, and they cannot pretend that home is a safe place when toddlers are taught to crawl to the bathroom at the sound of gunfire or when outdoor play is restricted out of fear of kidnapping. Weapons and assaults are common events in schools. Students and teachers share fears of what may erupt over minor disagreements. The schools can't guarantee the safety of either their students or their teachers.

Garbarino, Dubrow, Kostelny, and Pardo (1992), summarizing theirs and others' research on children and violence, identify the variety of trauma-reactive behaviors manifested by children exposed to violence. Age makes a difference. Those exposed to traumatizing violence before the age of eleven are three times more likely to develop psychiatric symptoms than those who experience their first trauma in their teens. Preschool children are more likely to show passivity and regression. School-age children typically show more aggression and more inhibition, as well as somatic, cognitive, and learning difficulties. Adolescents may engage in acting-out and self-destructive behaviors.

The trauma of violence interrupts and distorts the developmental process at every age. As Garbarino notes, the damage increases with the level of stress in a child's environment. All responses to the trauma of violence impede a child's ability to learn. As a result, finding a way to help children cope with violence has become a necessary task of educators. Finding ways of making the school a secure, stable, and safe environment is another essential task. Helping children learn that alternatives to violence exist and that they can choose to use such alternatives is yet another.

Classroom teachers are not the only ones confronting the effects of violence on children. Health educators and public health officials share a need to prevent violence that affects children and youth. The firearm homicide rate for youths aged ten to fourteen more than doubled between 1985 and 1992 (Carnegie Council on Adolescent Development, 1995, p. 24). Those startling statistics have given birth to the notion of dealing with violence as a public health issue for children. As with many health initiatives, the approach that makes the most sense is one of prevention. In *Deadly Consequences* and its accompanying violence prevention curriculum, Deborah Prothro-Stith and Michaela Weissman (1991) take a public health approach to the problem of youth violence. The U.S. Office of Disease Prevention and Health Promotion has included violence prevention as a primary objective in its *Health for the Year 2000: Objectives for the Nation.*

Conflict resolution skills provide ways of seeing and responding to conflicts with peers from a position of empowerment and confidence rather than with violence. Robert Selman, of Harvard University's Graduate School of Education, points out that children's interpersonal relationships in school predict their future personal adjustment. Acquiring conflict resolution skills in the early school years helps children learn effective problem solving. Research by Nancy Carlsson-Paige and Diane E. Levin (1992) suggests that the process of constructing an understanding of conflict and how to resolve it is a slow one, because children must use what they see around them to build their sense of how people treat others. New learnings build on prior experiences. Carlsson-Paige and Levin's research on the effect of violent cartoons on children's conflict behaviors (1991) revealed the damaging influence of negative role models as children are developing their conflict expression and resolution behaviors.

Julie Lam (1989), in her review of evaluation data on conflict resolution programs in schools, found three research projects that looked at the impact of conflict resolution on aggression. These projects (in Tucson, Arizona; New York City; and Poughkeepsie, New York) examined aggression, suspensions for fighting, and student reports of choosing not to fight. All showed positive trends. While such data is far from conclusive, it does—along with other assessments by students, teachers, and administrators of changes in self-esteem, school climate, and student conflict management skills—support the value of including conflict resolution programs in schools as one component of a violence prevention program.

Critical Thinking

A basic task of our educational programs, at every level, is to teach students to think. Skills in analysis, hypothesizing, predicting, strategizing, summarizing, comparing, communicating, and choosing are central to most academic subjects. Learning to solve problems is a task of the toddler as well as the eighth-grader; therefore, guiding that learning is the focus of both the preschool teacher and the high school teacher. Education in conflict resolution not only helps students develop critical thinking skills, it also applies them to students' concrete experiences.

Johnson and Johnson (1989) describe constructive controversy as a means of promoting both academic learning and conflict resolution skills. Constructive controversy, which brings critical thinking and conflict resolution skills together in a specific teaching method, entails guiding students in a process of taking positions (in cooperative pairs), reversing positions, and seeking consensus to produce an agreed-upon position statement. Approaches such as this demonstrate how elements of conflict resolution can be integrated with critical thinking in classrooms in a variety of ways (Deutsch, 1986).

Site-Based Management

Site-based management is the current term for increasing democratic participation in school governance. Site-based management seeks to place decision-making activity "on site"—that is, as close to the consequence of the decision as possible. Far from a fad, its roots go back to the early progressive education movement, which acknowledged a link between the goals of education and the structure of schools. At that time, simply meeting with teachers to discuss curriculum and practices was a break with the tradition of "principal as czar." Frances Parker and other early progressive educators who held to the value of democratic processes in the schools were early models.

Today, the democratic decision-making reforms under way in site-based management initiatives are more comprehensive. They include new decision makers, representative bodies, the sharing of previously closely held information, and new roles for teachers, parents, and administrators. While teachers, parents, and administrators could benefit from conflict resolution skills anyway, to handle their existing decision-making and communication responsibilities, these skills are even more vital to effective management of such extensive change. As schools move toward shared decision-making models, conflicts over expectations, efficiency, vested and competing interests, information, rewards, resources, roles, and positions are likely to increase, even as the potential for greater satisfaction with shared power and participation grows. Conflict resolution offers a framework for those involved in moving to site-based management, including practical skills not only for managing conflicts but for improving decision making.

Implementing Conflict Resolution Education in Schools _____

Conflict resolution education can be implemented by schools in several ways. They can establish peer mediation programs. They can include conflict resolution information and skills in lesson plans. Staff development and parent education programs can include training in conflict resolution techniques. Teachers' classroom management style can reflect conflict resolution principles and approaches, as can site-based decision-making initiatives. These various approaches can be divided into three major categories: conflict resolution in the classroom, school-based mediation, and site-based decision-making models. Although schools do not always institute a comprehensive approach that includes all three categories, programs have often grown from one element (like a peer mediation program) to include developmentally appropriate curriculum for all students and training for teachers, administrators, and other school staff.

Conflict resolution skills can be taught through the standard curriculum in social studies, language arts, health education, citizenship education, and even math. In literature courses, during discussions about assigned readings, students might be asked to analyze the underlying causes of conflicts between characters and to suggest ways these conflicts could be resolved. Stories at all ages and reading levels, from *Dumbo* to *Romeo and Juliet*, can provoke constructive discussions and learning about conflict resolution. Likewise, social studies students may study a historical or contemporary conflict and use available information to role-play the negotiation of the conflict. In math classes, teachers have linked math and conflict resolution skills in story problems. For example, a story problem might describe a delinquent loan between friends and the financial needs of both parties. The solution would require students to come up with a plan that would take into account the interests of both parties as well as the mathematical calculations for repayment. When conflict resolution is incorporated into lesson plans in these ways, students begin to understand and analyze conflict; recognize the role of perceptions and biases; identify feelings, escalating factors, and common interests; and improve their skills in seeing multiple solutions and win-win possibilities.

Conflict resolution can also inform a teacher's classroom management style. The teacher sets the tone for the classroom. Teachers who consistently structure and support a nonthreatening environment in which cooperation is encouraged, trust is demonstrated, and group dialogue is frequent are important role models. They also provide students with opportunities to practice and reasons to choose nonviolent conflict resolution strategies over aggression and violence.

Another facet of the in-class model is teaching students how to solve their own disputes. With the aid of age-appropriate materials, teachers can demonstrate various problem-solving methods and the skills necessary to constructively resolve simple peer conflicts. While the reason for wanting to teach conflict resolution is often concern about school violence, violence prevention is often presented as an independent effort with its own curriculum and activities. At the same time, there are materials that incorporate conflict resolution strategies into a violence prevention initiative. Prothro-Stith and Weissman's *Deadly Consequences* (1991) and Creighton and Kivel's *Helping Teens Stop Violence* (1992) are two examples of violence prevention curricula.

Student peer mediation programs use trained students to guide disputing students through the mediation process. The student mediators are typically instructed by professional mediation trainers. Mediations may be scheduled and conducted in a designated "mediation room," or they may take place when and where the dispute arises—on the playground, in the hallway, or in the lunchroom. Peer mediation programs handle disputes involving jealousies, rumors, misunderstandings, bullying, fights, and personal property. They may, when appropriate, handle bias-related incidents involving racism, sexism, homophobia, anti-Semitism, or other forms of prejudice. However, student mediators do not take on conflicts involving drugs, weapons, or abuse.

To make peer mediation programs work, it is necessary for the whole school community—teachers, staff, parents, and students—to understand and make a commitment to the principles being taught. The development of a common language, with respect to conflict and its resolution, among all constituent groups of the school community is an important ingredient in program success and longevity.

In some schools, the mediation program is extended to include adults. Adult mediation programs can be established to handle conflicts between adults and sometimes between students and teachers. These programs require providing adults with mediation training similar to that given to students. A variety of conflicts, including personality clashes, disagreements over disciplinary actions, development of programming for children with special needs, truancy, and disputes related to cultural differences can be mediated in such programs.

Schools across the country are increasingly using collaborative site-based decision making to develop strategies for creating schools of high quality. This is a collaborative consensus-building approach for determining a school's goals and making decisions about how to achieve them. The underlying principle is that everyone affected by a decision must be involved or represented in making the decision. The result of this approach is a structure that allows direct or representative participation by teachers, administrators, students, and parents in setting policies and procedures related to the academic climate and program. Adults who will be participating can be trained in conflict resolution skills to benefit communication, decision-making processes, and overall management of such extensive organizational change.

Each of these ways of applying conflict resolution in the schools requires a different level of teacher training, of personal and professional commitment on the part of the teacher, and of participation from others in the school community. For example, integrating conflict resolution concepts into the existing curriculum does demand a basic understanding of conflict and conflict resolution approaches. At the same time, to the extent that conflict resolution is incorporated into other primary subjects and thus becomes part of the background curriculum, the level of teacher commitment to teaching conflict resolution skills can vary. Under that approach, a teacher's commitment to conflict resolution principles may not be visible to students. Also, in most settings this approach would not require support or approval from outside the classroom.

Incorporating principles of conflict resolution into classroom management demands that teachers have the opportunity to develop fluency in using collaborative, age-appropriate problem-solving strategies. Since effective classroom management depends at least in part on consistency, teachers should implement only those principles and practices that they are likely to be able to maintain. While classroom management approaches are not generally negotiated between teachers, younger children can be vulnerable to the discontinuities in teacher approaches, and conflicts can erupt between teachers over differences in classroom discipline. Therefore, depending on the situation, some discussion with one's professional peers may be an important component in implementing a classroom management style that includes conflict resolution processes.

Teaching students how to resolve disputes requires additional training in conflict resolution processes and a greater commitment, since it entails moving the subject to the foreground. In some instances, administrative or departmental approval may be necessary. Implementing a violence prevention curriculum also requires special training and the commitment of other teachers and administrators.

Implementing a student peer mediation program requires the training and cooperation of teachers and administrators. While one teacher may serve as an initial catalyst, such a program needs broad support and involvement. It also requires substantial funding. Therefore, this is not likely to be the application approach taken by new teachers or those without substantial experience in conflict resolution.

Support for building conflict resolution education into our schools can start with the pre-service preparation of teachers, counselors, and administrators. It can be furthered by courses offered at the graduate level, special certificate programs, and in-service training programs. Schools and departments of education can play a major role in guiding educators in the development of conflict resolution understanding, skills, and implementation plans.

Planning for Conflict Resolution in Schools

Clearly, education students, experienced teachers, counselors, and administrators all have many options to consider in thinking about the applications of conflict resolution principles to their profession. All educators can benefit from considering the potential value of conflict resolution skills in daily professional interactions—in managing conflicts with colleagues, parents, supervisors, and others. Educators can also benefit from considering the potential contribution of conflict resolution techniques to meeting goals for students, whether those goals are within the formal curriculum or are part of schoolwide goals supported by administrative and counseling personnel as well as classroom teachers. Where the overall school climate needs attention, educators may consider ways in which conflict resolution activities might improve conditions.

Decisions about implementing conflict resolution strategies involve complex considerations. Selecting an initial focus involves weighing personal interests and skills, students' needs, school climate and needs, and available time and resources. Goals, approaches, time lines, and implementation steps may need development. In an emerging field, even a burgeoning one, careful planning and well-articulated rationales for decisions are needed; they are needed in education not only to provide solid guidance for teachers' efforts but also to ensure that the basis for learning and dialogue is built into the conflict resolution field as it grows from teacher to teacher and school to school. Assisting educators with the process of finding the right fit between conflict resolution and their professional goals, responsibilities, and skills is an emerging role for those working with pre-service and in-service teachers, administrators, and counselors.

Planning for Conflict Resolution in Teacher Education

Schools and departments of education must also decide where conflict resolution fits into the professional preparation curriculum. Given the different ways conflict resolution can be applied in schools, each faculty member or group must determine both what they would like to see accomplished with respect to a conflict resolution curriculum and what they believe is initially possible. Each institution planning to incorporate conflict resolution in teacher education has a unique set of circumstances, determined by student population profiles, departmental and institutional decision-making structures, state credentialing requirements, core curricula, course sequences, and unit requirements. Differences in professional preparation curricula, leadership roles, and personal interests also contribute to the unique challenge faced by faculty and administrators interested in integrating conflict resolution into their programs.

Just as conflict resolution can be integrated into schools in many different ways, so can it be incorporated into professional preparation programs by means of either small or expansive initiatives. It can be included as part of pre-service preparation, graduate programs, or in-service training. Conflict resolution can be taught as a part of methods, classroom-management, health, counseling, communication, or administrative classes. It can be included within a course in as little as an hour, with the goal of introducing an awareness of conflict resolution as an emerging field, or in a longer segment that allows for an exploration of some of its foundational concepts and skills. It can be a separate one-unit or three-unit course, or a full certificate program. The planning of new courses or course elements in an emerging field requires an emphasis on the considerations underlying our decisions. In the late 1980s and early 1990s, substantial pressure has been placed on the teacher education curriculum—any additions must be carefully weighed and justified. Institutions engaged in incorporating conflict resolution into their professional preparation programs will be looked to as models for others, both in terms of what was added and in terms of how the change was introduced and approved. Since implementation plans and decisions may have an impact far beyond a single college or university, it is important for faculty to articulate the thinking behind their approach.

As part of developing a conscious plan for teaching conflict resolution, faculty should consider realistically assessing both potential barriers to and strategies for successful implementation. Such assessments can only enhance the success of efforts to include conflict resolution in the professional preparation program, and they may also have a substantial impact on how conflict resolution unfolds in the field. Careful documentation of early efforts will provide an important resource for sharing ideas on conflict resolution with colleagues at other institutions.

Finally, given the time lag that invariably occurs between an idea and its actual implementation, careful planning becomes a crucial component. Defining the steps to be taken, when they will occur, and who is responsible for what actions can provide a necessary link between planning and implementation and can serve as an important support in seeing a new program through to successful operation.

The experiences of the eleven colleges and universities participating in the Conflict Resolution in Teacher Education Project reflected both the importance of planning and the way in which circumstances determine choices about course and unit design. Some faculty teams were able to incorporate conflict resolution into the next semester's courses. Others planned to introduce conflict resolution material in the following academic year. Some incorporated it into existing courses. For example, one faculty member developed a two-week conflict resolution module in the course Psychological Foundations of School Counseling. Another integrated it into a course, Discipline and Classroom Management for the

In-service Teacher, that combined twenty-five hours on conflict resolution skills with material on cooperative discipline. Still another faculty member incorporated material on intercultural conflict and conflict resolution into a course called Minorities in Education. Other courses into which conflict resolution was added included Adolescent Development, Organization and Administration, School Health, Classroom Management, and Student Teaching.

In addition to integrating conflict resolution education into other courses, faculty have also developed complete courses on conflict resolution. A few of these are described briefly below:

- *Conflict Resolution.* The University of Northern Iowa has developed a survey of social science, research, and theory as it applies to conflict resolution, using both theoretical frameworks and experiential learning.

- *Introduction to Conflict Resolution for the Student Teacher.* The University of Delaware has developed this new seminar option for students prior to their first school assignment.

- *Violence Prevention Strategies for Schools.* Emporia State University in Kansas has developed this program of discussion, ideas, and strategies for coping with violence and conflict in schools.

- *Course Sequence.* Texas Wesleyan University has developed four graduate courses as part of a new specialization in conflict resolution. These courses include Conflict Resolution, Negotiation, Mediation, and System Design in Schools (Conflict Resolution).

The material in this manual can be used in many ways to support courses in conflict resolution of varying degrees of depth and complexity. See Appendix F for some possible approaches to the subject.

References

Carlsson-Paige, N., & Levin, D. E. (1991, Winter). "The subversion of healthy development and play: What teachers say about the Teenage Mutant Ninja Turtles." *Day Care and Early Education,* p. 9, N2.

Carlsson-Paige, N., & Levin, D. E. (1992, November). "Making peace in violent times: A constructive approach to conflict resolution. *Young Children,* p. 4, N1.

Carnegie Council on Adolescent Development (1995). *Great transitions: Preparing adolescents for a new century.* New York: The Carnegie Corporation.

Creighton, A., & Kivel, P. (1992). *Helping teens stop violence.* Alameda, CA: Hunter House.

Deutsch, M. (1986). *Conflict resolution: Theory and practice.* Amherst, MA: National Association for Mediation in Education.

Deutsch, M. (1991). *Educating for a peaceful world.* Amherst, MA: National Association for Mediation in Education.

Dewey, J. (1949). *The school and society.* Chicago: University of Chicago Press.

Garbarino, J., Dubrow, N., Kostelny, K., & Pardo, C. (1992). *Children in danger: Coping with the consequences of community violence.* San Francisco: Jossey-Bass.

Jackson, D. (Director). (1988). *Solving conflicts* [videotape]. (Available from Churchill Media, 6901 Woodley Avenue, Van Nuys, CA 91406).

Johnson, D. W., & Johnson, R. T. (1989). *Cooperation and competition: Theory and research.* Edina, MN: Interaction Book Company.

Lam, J. (1989). *The impact of conflict resolution programs on schools: A review and synthesis of the evidence.* Amherst, MA: National Association for Mediation in Education.

Prothro-Stith, D., & Weissman, M. (1991). *Deadly consequences: How violence is destroying our teenage population and a plan to begin solving the problem.* New York: HarperCollins.

Exercises

The purpose of these exercises is to deepen students' understanding of the ways conflict resolution fits into education theory and practice and, perhaps, to stimulate further exploration of these issues.

 ## Exercise 4.1. Conflict Resolution in the Schools

NOTE: This exercise provides instructors and students with an opportunity for extensive discussion of—and perhaps additional research on—the background section of this module.

Objectives

- Explore the various ways in which conflict resolution theory and skills support the fundamental goals of our educational system
- Explore the ways in which conflict resolution theory and skills address current issues and concerns in our public schools

Procedures

1. Guide a discussion about how conflict resolution fits into the public schools. How does it fit with general educational aims? What current concerns and needs might it address? What other educational trends does it fit with? Draw upon the ideas outlined in the Background section to prompt thinking. Allow forty-five minutes to an hour for the discussion. *Note:* Exhibit 4.1, NAME's "Ten Reasons for Implementing Conflict Resolution Programs in Schools," is a useful tool for this discussion.

Exhibit 4.1.   **Ten Reasons for Implementing Conflict Resolution Programs in Schools**

A review of program descriptions reveals that the following reasons most commonly motivate those who wish to promote mediation in the schools.

1. Conflict is a natural human state often accompanying changes in our institutions or personal growth. It is better approached with skills than avoidance.

2. More appropriate and effective systems are needed to deal with conflict in the school setting than expulsion, suspension, court intervention and detention.

3. The use of mediation to resolve school-based disputes can result in improved communication between and among students, teachers, administrators and parents and can, in general, improve the school climate as well as provide a forum for addressing common concerns.

4. The use of mediation as a conflict resolution method can result in a reduction of violence, vandalism, chronic school absence and suspension.

5. Mediation training helps both young people and teachers deepen their understanding about themselves and others and provides them with lifetime dispute resolution skills.

6. Mediation training increases students' interest in conflict resolution, justice, and the American legal system while encouraging a higher level of citizenship activity.

7. Shifting the responsibility for solving appropriate school conflicts from adults to young adults and children frees both teachers and administrators to concentrate more on teaching than on discipline.

8. Recognizing that young people are competent to participate in the resolution of their own disputes encourages student growth and gives students skills—such as listening, critical thinking, and problem solving—that are basic to all learning.

9. Mediation training, with its emphasis upon listening to others' points of view and the peaceful resolution of differences, assists in preparing students to live in a multicultural world.

10. Mediation provides a system of problem solving that is uniquely suited to the personal nature of young people's problems and is frequently used by students for problems they would not take to parents, teachers or principals.

Source: Davis, A., & Porter, K. (1985). "Tales of schoolyard mediation." *UPDATE on Law-Related Education, 9,* 27. Reprinted by permission.

Exercise 4.2. Building Rationales for Conflict Resolution

NOTE: This exercise provides students with an opportunity to develop and view the implementation of conflict resolution programs in schools from various constituency perspectives.

Objective

- Develop a rationale for including conflict resolution in the schools

Procedures

1. Have the class split up into four equal groups, and ask each group to assume one of the roles listed in this step. You can either assign the roles or let the groups choose, as long as all four of these roles are covered:

- An elementary school teacher talking to parents
- A high school teacher talking to the principal
- A superintendent talking to the school board
- A university professor talking to education students

2. Ask the groups to work from the point of view of their assumed role as they develop rationales for teaching conflict resolution in the schools. Have them outline their main points on chart paper for display and presentation to the whole group. Allow thirty minutes for this step.

3. Have the groups present their outlines, and discuss any differences in rationale based on audience, age of students, and position in the education system of the role they played. Did the groups' rationales reflect their members' personal rationales for pursuing conflict resolution? Allow thirty minutes for discussion.

Exercise 4.3. Teachable Moments

NOTE: Teachable moments are those times when an educator transforms an unplanned event (sometimes a difficult one!) in a classroom or other school setting into a learning opportunity. Conflict in classrooms and schools present lots of "teachable moments."

Objectives

- Explore the ways in which conflict resolution theory and skills address current issues and concerns in the public schools
- Establish a personal vision for the participants' place and work in the field of conflict resolution in education.

Procedures

1. Screen the video *Solving Conflicts* (Jackson, 1988).

2. After the participants view the video, lead a discussion of the following points:

- What skills enabled the teacher to intervene effectively?
- What might prevent educators from developing these skills?
- What would support educators in developing these skills?

3. If possible, bring in a guest presenter (or more than one) who has experience coordinating school conflict resolution programs. We have found this to be very useful; it gives the participants one or two hours to have an interactive discussion with an experienced provider of school conflict resolution programs.

Exercise 4.4. Planning for Implementation of Conflict Resolution by Pre-Service Education Students

NOTE: Most pre-service educators identify their lack of preparation for handling classroom conflict as a serious concern. This exercise will help educators develop short- and long-term conflict resolution strategies to take into their in-service practice.

Objectives

- Identify the desired goals to be met through the incorporation of conflict resolution into professional life
- Identify the best means to achieve these goals
- Identify practical criteria that will affect the goals and approach that are finally selected and implemented
- Develop a rationale for including conflict resolution in the schools
- Identify potential barriers to implementing conflict resolution in professional activities, curricula, or instruction, and explore possible ways to overcome them
- Identify the development and implementation steps—including any further training, assistance, or approval by others—that will be required to introduce and practice conflict resolution in the schools

Procedures

1. Lead a discussion of the range or continuum of ways that teachers, counselors, and administrators can incorporate conflict resolution in their work (for example, from "bring awareness of conflict resolution communication skills to dealings with colleagues, parents, and supervisors" to "teach conflict resolution skills to my students" to "infuse conflict resolution approaches throughout the school").

2. Allow participants to identify where they would place themselves on the continuum, and then form small groups or pairs around these placements.

3. Have the pairs or small groups develop answers to the following questions for each of their members:

    a. What goals would I want to achieve over three years?

    b. What goals could I achieve over one year?

    c. What resources (additional training, institutional support, collegial support, and so forth) would I need to achieve these goals?

    d. What activities would be necessary as part of achieving these goals?

    e. Who would be likely to support these efforts?

    f. Who might oppose these efforts?

    g. Are there any risks in trying to achieve these goals?

    h. Are there ways to eliminate or minimize these risks?

4. Reassemble the large group and discuss the exercise. Depending on the number of groups and the size of the groups, have one or two students from each group present answers to the questions, allowing time for other students to ask questions and make suggestions.

5. Have students complete the implementation contract (Exhibit 4.2).

Exhibit 4.2.   Implementation Contract

NAME: _____

DATE: _____

GOALS: As a _____, I intend to achieve the following goals related to conflict resolution:

_____

_____

_____

_____

_____

In order to achieve these goals, I commit to doing the following within the next year:

_____

_____

_____

_____

_____

I will need to overcome the following obstacles:

_____

_____

_____

_____

_____

I will seek help and support from:

_____

_____

_____
Signature

Glossary

Active listening: A communication procedure in which the listener uses nonverbal behaviors, such as eye contact and gestures, as well as verbal behaviors, including tone of voice, open-ended questioning, restating, and summarizing, to demonstrate to the speaker that the listener is paying attention.

Agenda: A list of items for discussion, such as issues or problem statements, assembled in a sequence that facilitates efficient discussion and problem solving.

Aggression: Forceful action or attack.

Arbitration: Intervention into a dispute by an independent third party who is given authority to collect information, listen to both sides, and make a decision as to how the conflict should be settled. Arbitration may be binding or nonbinding.

Assessment: An evaluation of a conflict situation. An assessment involves investigation of the parties; their interests, positions, needs, and power; settlement options; and other factors that impact the situation.

Avoidance: The practice of nonengagement.

Basic needs: Needs that underlie all human behavior—survival, self-worth, belonging, self-actualization, power, freedom, fun. Like individuals, groups also have basic needs, including the need for identity, security, vitality, and community.

BATNA: An acronym for Best Alternative to a Negotiated Agreement, the standard against which any proposed agreement is measured.

Bias: A preconceived opinion or attitude about something or someone. A bias may be favorable or unfavorable.

Brainstorming: Literally, a storm of ideas. A group-thinking technique for helping disputants create multiple options for consideration in solving a problem. Brainstorming separates the creative act from the critical one—all criticism and evaluation of ideas is postponed until later.

Caucus: A private meeting held between mediator(s) and disputant(s) to discuss needs and interests, the negotiating plan, and ways to make the procedure more productive.

Clarify: To make clearer or to enhance understanding. During a conflict resolution procedure, open-ended questions are often used to clarify meaning.

Collaboration: Working with the other side to seek solutions that completely satisfy both parties. This involves accepting both parties' concerns as valid and digging into an issue in an attempt to find innovative possibilities. It also means being open and exploratory.

Common interests or *common ground:*   Needs and/or interests that are identified as being held jointly by the parties in a negotiation.

Community: A group that has common interests, a common identity, and common customs.

Competition: A strategy by which one pursues the satisfaction of one's own interests at the expense of others—a win-lose approach.

Compromise: An expedient settlement that only partially satisfies both sides. Compromising doesn't dig into the underlying problem, but rather seeks a more superficial arrangement such as "splitting the difference." It is based upon partial concessions—giving up something to get something—and may be played "close to the vest" (with an underlying competitive attitude).

Conflict: An expressed struggle between at least two interdependent parties who perceive incompatible goals, scarce resources, and interference from the other party in achieving their goals; a controversy or disagreement; to come into opposition.

Conflict resolution: A spectrum of processes that utilize communication skills and creative thinking to develop voluntary solutions that are acceptable to those concerned in a dispute. Conflict resolution processes include negotiation (between two parties), mediation (involving a third-party process guide) and consensus building (facilitated group decision making).

Consensus: An agreement reached by identifying the interests of all concerned parties and then building an integrative solution that maximizes satisfaction of as many of their interests as possible; a synthesis and blending of solutions.

Consequence: A result that logically follows an action.

Cooperation: Associating for mutual benefit; working toward a common end or purpose.

Culture: That part of human interactions and experiences that determines how people feel, act, and think. It is through one's culture that one establishes standards to judge right from wrong, beauty and truth, and the worth of oneself and others. Culture includes one's nationality, ethnicity, race, gender, sexual orientation, socioeconomic background, ability, and age.

De-escalate: To engage in actions that decrease the intensity of a conflict.

Disputant: One who is engaged in a disagreement or conflict.

Diversity: A term used to refer to individual differences and racial, ethnic, or cultural differences.

Empowerment: A method of balancing power in a relationship, wherein the party with the lesser power is provided more power by gaining expertise, being provided extra resources, building interpersonal linkages, and/or enhancing his or her communication skills.

Escalate: To engage in particular actions that increase the intensity of a conflict.

Evaluation: The assessment of an option or possible conflict solution.

Facilitator: A third party or parties who provide procedural assistance to a group attempting to reach consensus about a problem.

Framing: The manner in which a conflict situation or issue is conceptualized or defined.

Ground rule: A basic rule of behavior spelled out and agreed to at the beginning of a conflict resolution procedure.

Hidden interest: A basic need or want that is not immediately evident in a conflict situation but that needs to surface and be addressed before meaningful dialogue can occur.

"I" message: A framework for communicating both meaning and emotion in a nonthreatening way. "I" messages take this form: "I feel ____ when ____ because ____, and I need ____." The last clause is optional.

Interest: A substantive, procedural, or psychological need of a party to a conflict; the aspect of something that makes it matter to someone.

Mediation: Intervention in a dispute by an impartial third party who can help the disputants negotiate an acceptable settlement.

Mediator: An invited intervener whose expertise and experience in conflict resolution techniques and processes is used to help disputants reach a satisfactory solution. The mediator is a process guide whose presence is acceptable to both disputants; he or she has no decision-making power to determine a settlement.

Negotiation: A relationship between two or more parties who have an actual or perceived conflict of interest. In a negotiation, the participants join voluntarily in a dialogue to educate one another about their needs and interests, exchange information, and create a solution that meets the needs of both sides.

Negotiation power: The ability to persuade someone to do something.

Option: An alternative course of action; a possible solution that may satisfy the interests of a party to a dispute.

Position: A point of view; a specific solution that a party proposes to meet his or her interests or needs. A position is likely to be concrete and explicit, and it often includes a demand or threat that leaves little room for discussion. In conflict resolution, an essential activity is for participants to get beyond their positions to understand their underlying interests and needs.

Power: The ability to act or perform effectively; the ability to influence others.

Reframing: The process of changing how a person or a party to a conflict conceptualizes his, her, or another's attitudes, behaviors, issues, and interests or how a situation is defined. Reframing during conflict resolution processes helps to mitigate defensiveness and de-escalate tension.

Resolution: A course of action agreed upon to solve a problem.

Restraint: A method of balancing power in a relationship, whereby the side with the greater power voluntarily declines to apply some of the power at its disposal.

Site-based management: A system of school district management that seeks democratic participation in decision making by parents, students, administrators, teachers, and other stakeholders at each local school.

Summarize: To restate in a brief, concise form. Summarizing is an aspect of active listening that is utilized by both disputants and mediators to increase common understanding.

Trust: To have confidence in or to feel sure of; faith.

Value: A principle, standard, or quality considered worthwhile or desirable.

Violence: The unjust or abusive use of power; force exerted for the purpose of injuring, damaging, or abusing people or property.

WATNA: An acronym for Worst Alternative to a Negotiated Settlement. What may happen if the disputants do not settle their differences.

Guidelines for
Conducting Role Plays

Role plays, in the form of negotiation and mediation simulations, scenarios, and tableaus, are important learning tools in conflict resolution education. Role playing is useful in helping participants to understand their behavior, as a method of skills development and process rehearsal, and as a step in conflict analysis. Like any other instructional method, role playing requires careful planning and clear linkage to instructional objectives.

Each step in role playing—*preparation, introduction, action,* and *processing*—is equally important if the activity is to meet its intended goal. The facilitator's responsibility is to clearly articulate the objectives and procedures and to manage the experience to best advantage.

Preparation

1. Before beginning a role-play exercise, consider the learning objectives and the appropriateness of using the role-play method as opposed to some other exercise.

2. Decide whether to develop your own role-play situation or to solicit them from participants. (Developing your own in advance provides the opportunity to more clearly delineate roles, predict outcomes, and control the activity. This may be the best choice with a less experienced group. Soliciting ideas from the participants in advance to allow for planning is often helpful and makes the expe-

rience more relevant and contemporary.) Appendix C provides several scenarios you can use or adapt to your purposes.

3. Select the situation, define the problem or issues to be considered, and develop necessary details. (The situation should be described in at least a brief paragraph.)

4. Identify and name the roles to be played, developing sufficient background for each role. (Roles should be described in a brief individual paragraph for each assigned player.) *Note:* It is often helpful for the processing phase to assign observers who can stay outside of the scene and later describe what they saw and understood.

5. Determine the procedure and time limits that best fit the exercise. Possible procedures include having small groups engaged in the same simulation, having one group perform for all, or having small groups engage in different scenarios.

6. Assemble any props and supplies that may contribute to the effectiveness of the role play (name tags, signs, and so on).

7. Develop process questions to be used after the action step. Process questions should elicit participant reactions and be tied clearly to lesson objectives.

Introduction

1. Describe the purpose of the role play to participants. Clearly link the exercise to learning objectives, unless the discovery of that link is part of what you want the participants to accomplish in the exercise.

2. Describe the situation briefly, distributing a written simulation description to all participants and observers.

3. Select the role players and distribute role descriptions and name tags. (Care should be taken to provide opportunities to volunteer for various roles. No one should feel forced to play a role that feels uncomfortable.) It is important for role players to assume their roles by putting on name tags and to take off the tags at the end of the role play. This clearly separates the participant from the role, an action that benefits both participants and observers.

4. Provide instructions for the actors:

   a. You will be allowed _____ minutes for planning and _____ minutes for performance. (It is useful to allow players a few minutes of planning time to review their role descriptions, go over the simulation, and agree on common facts implied in the scenario.)

   b. Consider this a learning opportunity for all.

c. Put yourself in the position of the individual described in the role description. Consider how that individual might feel, look, and act. Stay in the role until the exercise is complete.

d. Do not change essential information given in the role and situation description (although you may elaborate and create details).

e. Do not share your role description with other players.

5. Provide instructions for observers:

a. Be specific about what the audience should watch for. (It is sometimes helpful to create a worksheet that requires certain observations. Use the questions in Exercise 3.5, number 3.)

b. Observe with the intention of providing positive and useful feedback.

6. Provide at least a brief opportunity for planning and rehearsal.

Action

1. Briefly set the scene by sharing the situation and the role descriptions.

2. Start the action. (If more than one group will perform a role play for an audience composed of several groups, request a volunteer group to perform first.)

3. Allow the role play to proceed with adequate time.

4. Intervene only if participants clearly need help. If an interruption is necessary, make a clear, concise suggestion, or ask a question to move the situation forward.

5. You may choose to call "Cut!" or "Freeze!" at a particular point in the action or at the end of the role play. Action should then stop immediately. At the end of the role play, applaud the participants and request that they remove their name tags and resume their own identity.

Processing

1. Ask the role players to comment first, describing why they chose to take particular actions and their feelings about their actions and those of others in the scene. Some helpful questions are

    a. What was the experience like for you?

    b. How did you feel when . . . ?

    c. Why did you choose a particular action?

    d. What did you learn?

    e. Are you satisfied with the outcome?

    f. If you were to do the role play again, what would you change?

2. Invite observers and audience members to discuss what they saw. Observers can provide positive feedback and attempt to analyze observed behavior, engaging the actors in dialogue about the situation. Observers should also be encouraged to comment on their own reactions and feelings about what took place. Some helpful questions are

    a. What did you observe?

    b. How did you feel when . . . ?

    c. Why do you think [character] chose a particular action?

    d. What did you learn?

    e. Are you satisfied with the outcome?

    f. If you had played a role, what would you have changed?

Note: Careful and thoughtful facilitation of the processing step is essential for reaching the lesson objective. Without processing, lesson objectives cannot be achieved, and the role play becomes meaningless playtime.

Role Play Examples

Following are a series of role plays provided to assist you in using Module Three, "Alternative Dispute Resolution Processes." We have also included a scenario called "Intercultural Case Study." The case study works well as a discussion piece and provides a base for exercises throughout the manual. You could also use it to develop your own mediation role plays.

Negotiation: Course Requirement Exemption (Faculty Advisor Role)

Situation Summary

Your department has a set of core courses required of all master's students, no matter what their specialization. The core requirements make up twelve units of the thirty-three-unit master's program. Faculty advisors have the authority to waive the requirement when they feel special circumstances, usually previous academic work, warrants an exemption. In this instance, a graduate student specializing in counseling wishes to be exempted from a required course, Philosophy of Education, although she has not had prior exposure to this set of ideas in an academic framework. The counseling program has twenty-one required units.

Background Information

Your advisee is a master's student in counseling. This student has completed all the core courses required by the department except for Philosophy of Education and has completed the first three courses in the counseling sequence. So far this student seems to be doing fine. She is maintaining a 3.8 average. The student has requested to see you to talk about the possibility of getting an exemption. Master's students often ask for exemptions to required departmental courses because the number of units is so limited and there are few or no opportunities for electives, depending on the specialization. However, it was agreed in the department to establish the core requirements, and there are budgetary as well as political and collegial-support issues that discourage advisors from being too easy in granting exemptions.

Faculty Advisor Role

You don't like the continual assault of elaborate stories, special circumstances, and desperate pleadings—all aimed at you with the intention of getting you to authorize an exemption, extend a deadline, or change a grade. You always make certain that the rules are clear to students at the outset so that they can take responsibility for their choices, their time, and their performance. You believe that this is important training for professional conduct in the world, and it is one of the things you try to impart to your students. You do not grant exemptions, extend deadlines, or change grades except in extremely rare cases. Not only do you not believe in it on principle, you don't want to do it to your colleagues. You wouldn't want them exempting students from your courses, thereby sending a message that your courses were not important and reducing the measures of your productivity in the eyes of the dean and the university.

Negotiation: Course Requirement Exemption (Graduate Student Role) _____

Situation Summary

Your department has a set of core courses required of all master's students, no matter what their specialization. The core requirements make up twelve units of the thirty-three-unit master's program. Faculty advisors have the authority to waive the requirement when they feel special circumstances, usually previous academic work, warrants an exemption. You are a graduate student specializing in counseling. You wish to be exempted from a required course, Philosophy of Education, although you have not had prior exposure to this set of ideas in an academic framework. The counseling program has twenty-one required units.

Student Background Information

You are a master's student in counseling with a special interest in adolescent drug and alcohol abuse counseling. The way the program is structured, you have no electives to use to take a course in drug and alcohol counseling. You cannot afford to add courses, since the thirty-three units is already putting you in more debt than you feel comfortable with. You're already halfway through the program. Philosophy of Education is the only core requirement you haven't completed. You developed the idea that drug and alcohol abuse counseling is the right focus for you in a class last semester.

Graduate Student Role

You want an exemption from the Philosophy of Education course. It does not seem relevant to you. It's the only core requirement you haven't met yet. You came to get a good education and preparation for counseling, and now you're being prevented from learning what you most need. The school talks about learner-centered education, and you want your education to be centered around what you need to learn. You think you're in the best position to know what you'll benefit from most. Besides, as an undergraduate you took philosophy, and you've already taken Ed Psych. A friend of yours got an exemption from Current Issues in Public Education, another core requirement.

Negotiation: George Washington (Jason's Teacher Role) _____

Situation Summary

Jason is in the fifth grade. He came to school today without his homework assignment, which was to write three paragraphs on George Washington. Jason had begun his work during class and was to finish it at home as the final activity in a recent history unit. Instead of his homework, Jason brought a note from his mother (or father) saying she would be at school at 3:00 P.M. and expected to meet with the teacher then.

Teacher Background Information

This is your second year of teaching. Last year you completed your master's, and you are very excited about the curriculum changes you've made this year. Your class on multicultural education was extremely valuable and has provided some excellent materials that you're using this year. For the first time you feel that you are able to offer something relevant to the African American children who make up almost half your class. In fact, you've just finished a unit that included looking at the "fathers" of America in terms of slavery. You particularly enjoyed being able to show George Washington as a hero on one hand but a slave owner on the other. You've always hated the ridiculous cherry tree story. You were proud of the way the children were able to ask questions about how someone could be both good and bad.

Teacher Role

You're not quite sure what Jason's mother wants to see you about. The note she sent with Jason just said that Jason had not been able to complete his assignment and that she would be in at 3:00. Jason has been quiet and withdrawn, and you haven't wanted to embarrass him by asking about what happened to his assignment. Jason's parents didn't come to the open house last month, so you haven't had a chance to meet them. You're a little nervous about the meeting and a little annoyed that she didn't ask if 3:00 would be convenient for you.

Negotiation: George Washington (Jason's Parent Role) _____

Situation Summary

Jason is in the fifth grade. He came to school today without his homework assignment, which was to write three paragraphs on George Washington. Jason had begun his work during class and was to finish it at home as the final activity in a recent history unit. Instead of his homework, Jason brought a note from his mother (or father) saying she would be at school at 3:00 P.M. and expected to meet with the teacher then.

Parent Background Information

Your family moved to this city and school system last year. It's been a change from the small rural town in which you grew up and began to raise your family. You're trying to adjust, but you find people unfriendly, abrasive, dishonest, and different. You used to know what people thought was important and what they valued, and you used to share those ideas and values with them. Now you feel positively alone. And you're afraid for your children. What ideas and values are they going to pick up? You believe the public schools should teach the basic American values that were taught when you were in school and that are still taught in your hometown. You were horrified to read your son's homework and find out that he was writing about George Washington as a "bad man who owned slaves." You learned that George Washington was a boy who never told a lie, and that seems a much more important lesson than this garbage about George Washington and slaves.

Parent Role

You want your son to receive the right kind of education, one that will instill in him a love of country and a wish to be a good citizen and be honest and truthful. You want him to have heroes. You are extremely upset with what this teacher is teaching. You are doing the courtesy of speaking with the teacher first, but your next stop is the principal. You want this curriculum changed.

Negotiation: Teaching Style
(American Government Teacher Role) _____

Situation Summary

A seventh-grade English teacher is concerned about the condition of some of her fourth-period students who come to class following American Government. She has sent a note to the American Government teacher asking to talk for a few minutes after the teachers' meeting about a couple of students. The American Government teacher agreed.

American Government Teacher Background Information

You've taught for thirty years at this school. You've seen times when kids really paid attention, worked hard, and wanted to be good citizens, and you've seen times, like now, when no one cares and you've got a lot of punks in your classes who represent the depths to which society is sinking. You've got three kids like that in your third-period class. At one point you thought about moving to the high school, where you could have taught political science and worked with really motivated kids, getting them involved in local and national programs related to democratic processes and politics. But you really enjoy the opportunity to make a difference in these formative years. If you can catch some of the kids early, maybe you can be a force to stop the erosion of our nation's moral fiber and bring back a sense of moral decency. You teach the kids about values, discipline, and excellence. You teach them about competing fairly and participating. You can be hard on the kids, but now is the time for them to either choose to be responsible or to learn that there are consequences for not being responsible.

American Government Teacher Role

You don't know this teacher who's asked to meet with you about some kids, but you're pleased to be asked to help. You're glad to see that your work is respected outside your department. You're excellent at imposing discipline and can offer some suggestions, or perhaps there's a way the English teacher wants to use government material in a unit. You're looking forward to this meeting and to helping the English teacher with her problem.

Negotiation: Teaching Style (English Teacher Role) _____

Situation Summary

A seventh-grade English teacher is concerned about the condition of some of her fourth-period students who come to class following American Government. She has sent a note to the American Government teacher asking to talk for a few minutes after the teachers' meeting about a couple of students. The American Government teacher agreed.

English Teacher Background Information

You have noticed that three students consistently seem "down in the dumps" when they come into your class. You've talked with them individually and have found out that they hate their American Government class, which is taught by a teacher with almost thirty years at the school. They are all pretty openly rebellious and seem into the "punk" scene. You gather that the American Government teacher routinely uses all three as examples of decay, decadence, and the collapse of morals in American society. You know these students can be difficult to deal with, but you feel you are reaching them with literature. You believe that embarrassing these students is inappropriate and detrimental to their development. You've seen students turn around, but through love and acceptance, not through ridicule. Your concern is that these kids are going to fail the government class and this will set them on a negative path that will become harder and harder to change.

English Teacher Role

You want to prevent further embarrassment and damage, and you do not want the American Government teacher to jeopardize the progress you have begun to make with these kids. You want to help the American Government teacher see the problem with his current approach. You want these kids to have successful school experiences.

Mediation: Budgetary Constraints
(Teacher Requesting the TV Role) _____

Situation Summary

Two members of the science department in a junior high school have submitted requests to their department chair. One teacher requested $900 for a new large-screen television and VCR to be dedicated to the science department. The other teacher requested $900 for a mobile lab, which would facilitate hands-on demonstrations and experiments. The chair submitted these requests to the principal, who, in turn, passed them on to the resource allocation committee. The resource allocation committee decided to expend the majority of funds available for materials on new ESL and multicultural texts for English and social studies classes. The science department chair was notified that there would only be $800 available for new science materials. The two science teachers do not see eye to eye on teaching methods, and the chair wants to avoid taking sides. The chair has asked the faculty union representative and one of the counselors to assist in mediating this conflict and to try to get an agreement from the two teachers. The two teachers have agreed to participate in this process.

Background Information for Teacher Requesting TV

You've been teaching at this junior high for seventeen years. The English department has its own TV and VCR, but you must share one with the social studies department. You use many videos in your teaching. Kids are used to that medium. They like movies and there are some excellent videos for introducing concepts, demonstrating experiments, and so on. Last year, you were only able to get the TV and VCR half the time you requested it. Other teachers in your department have the same complaint. Ideally, you'd like one in your classroom all the time. Your newest colleague, who has requested the mobile lab, has made snide remarks about the use of videos, or so you've been told—but kids request your class.

Teacher Requesting TV Role

Your request for the TV and VCR will benefit everyone in the department. It will benefit the department for many years. You do not want to have to endure another year of last-minute scrambling for activities because the equipment isn't there or is broken. You're an experienced teacher with department seniority. That should

count for something in deciding what gets funded. You've carefully priced available makes and models and have identified the TV
and VCR that should stand up to heavy use with a minimum of
maintenance. You've checked with the AV department, and they
concur with your recommendation.

Mediation: Budgetary Constraints
(Teacher Requesting Lab Role) _____

Situation Summary

Two members of the science department in a junior high school have submitted requests to their department chair. One teacher requested $900 for a new large-screen television and VCR to be dedicated to the science department. The other teacher requested $900 for a mobile lab, which would facilitate hands-on demonstrations and experiments. The chair submitted these requests to the principal, who, in turn, passed them on to the resource allocation committee. The resource allocation committee decided to expend the majority of funds available for materials on new ESL and multicultural texts for English and social studies classes. The science department chair was notified that there would only be $800 available for new science materials. The two science teachers do not see eye to eye on teaching methods, and the chair wants to avoid taking sides. The chair has asked the faculty union representative and one of the counselors to assist in mediating this conflict and to try to get an agreement from the two teachers. The two teachers have agreed to participate in this process.

Background Information for Teacher Requesting Lab

You've been teaching at this junior high school for two years. You are appalled by the lack of hands-on opportunities for kids. There are simply no materials for conducting experiments or for doing dissections, either as demonstrations or as individual and group activities. Teachers in this school tend to use texts and videos and assign term papers. You have not gotten much support from the department chair, who doesn't want to take on her teachers. You have talked with the district science coordinator, who would like to see more hands-on work with the children. You've recommended purchase of a mobile lab so that other teachers might be encouraged to use it. The district coordinator said they could provide training for the whole faculty in working with the lab. You've tested out other teachers' interest and have tried to suggest that videos are not really the best way to teach science, but no one really listens to you.

Teacher Requesting Lab Role

You were trained to teach in an active, discovery-based way. You are desperate for a lab and lab materials. You feel you are not teaching well and failing the kids because you don't have the materials you need. The least expensive lab setup you could find was $900. While it's far from ideal, it would be a start. You're losing kids from your classes, and you fear you're losing kids from science. You have so much to offer, and you're being prevented from offering it. You really need this lab.

Mediation: Teacher Grievance (Department Chair Role) _____

Situation Summary

A teacher with eighteen years at a high school has experienced numerous disputes with the school's science department chair, who has been there ten years (four as chair and six teaching), over the department's curriculum, particularly the sex education curriculum. This curriculum was adopted by the state, but it remains somewhat controversial because it addresses such subjects as masturbation, AIDS, safe sex, and homosexuality. Angry words and raised voices have occurred between the two educators. Finally, the department head included a very negative letter of reprimand with the teacher's annual evaluation. The teacher has demanded that the letter be rescinded. The department head has refused. The teacher has contacted the union representative about filing a grievance. The first step in the grievance process is to attempt mediation. The principal and union representative have met with both parties, who have agreed on two mediators from outside the department. If mediation does not resolve the problem, the next step in the formal grievance process will be taken.

Background Information

The letter the department head wrote states, "Your conduct over the past two years has been difficult, uncooperative, and unprofessional. Your recent meeting with parents concerning the department's sex education curriculum, which resulted in a protest at the board of education meeting, requires an official reprimand. It is expected that teachers will express their opinions in professional arenas and as private citizens, but your exploitation of parent fears for your own purposes is quite another matter. If you believe that curriculum material is not developmentally or morally appropriate, then you must take that up with me. If we cannot reach agreement, then it is appropriate for you to go to the principal. It is unprofessional and unethical for you to mobilize parents against the school in an attempt to achieve your personal and sectarian religious goals. I sincerely hope that you take this letter to heart and revisit your past actions in light of the responsibility you have as an educator in this school. Our task must be to serve our children and their parents, not our own interests."

Department Chair Role

You have had it. You have put up with this teacher's working behind the scenes against you for the four years you've chaired the department. Now this teacher has parents calling you immoral. You care deeply about the welfare of children and families, and you feel this teacher's actions could be harmful. You want to see this teacher contained or, better, gone. Other teachers seem intimidated because this teacher appears to use innuendo with parents and others in the district to suggest that those who disagree are morally suspect. You think the teacher is supported by the right-wing fundamentalists who recently campaigned for a candidate for the school board. Their candidate lost by a very small margin.

Mediation: Teacher Grievance (Teacher Role) _____

Situation Summary

A teacher with eighteen years at a high school has experienced numerous disputes with the school's science department chair, who has been there ten years (four as chair and six teaching), over the department's curriculum, particularly the sex education curriculum. This curriculum was adopted by the state, but it remains somewhat controversial because it addresses such subjects as masturbation, AIDS, safe sex, and homosexuality. Angry words and raised voices have occurred between the two educators. Finally, the department head included a very negative letter of reprimand with the teacher's annual evaluation. The teacher has demanded that the letter be rescinded. The department head has refused. The teacher has contacted the union representative about filing a grievance. The first step in the grievance process is to attempt mediation. The principal and union representative have met with both parties, who have agreed on two mediators from outside the department. If mediation does not resolve the problem, the next step in the formal grievance process will be taken.

Background Information

The letter the department head wrote states, "Your conduct over the past two years has been difficult, uncooperative, and unprofessional. Your recent meeting with parents concerning the department's sex education curriculum, which resulted in a protest at the board of education meeting, requires an official reprimand. It is expected that teachers will express their opinions in professional arenas and as private citizens, but your exploitation of parent fears for your own purposes is quite another matter. If you believe that curriculum material is not developmentally or morally appropriate, then you must take that up with me. If we cannot reach agreement, then it is appropriate for you to go to the principal. It is unprofessional and unethical for you to mobilize parents against the school in an attempt to achieve your personal and sectarian religious goals. I sincerely hope that you take this letter to heart and revisit your past actions in light of the responsibility you have as an educator in this school. Our task must be to serve our children and their parents, not our own interests."

Teacher Role

This letter will be removed. You will not have your exemplary record of teaching marred. You have a lot of power as a senior

teacher in the school and in the community. You have First Amend-
ment rights. Parents have a right to know about what the school is
teaching. You have the support of your minister and many people
in the community who believe children should not be exposed to
sexual material. Children need to be encouraged to stay away from
sex, not taught about it and encouraged to experiment. You care
deeply about the welfare of children and families. You believe in
keeping children children, not in turning them into adults prematurely. The department chair has lost sight of the values of the
majority of the community and of American society.

Mediation: Faculty Personnel Committee
(Advocate for Increasing Diversity Role) _____

Situation Summary

A recent accreditation report recommended that your institution take steps to provide greater diversity on its faculty. The school of education was specifically mentioned as needing policies to improve the recruitment and hiring of qualified faculty from under-represented groups. The dean has asked the personnel committee to draft guidelines for these policies quickly, since a search must be begun ASAP for a tenure-track position. The personnel committee has had one meeting. That meeting ended badly. The committee was split around the question of selection standards. Members accused each other of racism, of favoring race over credentials and competency, of protecting an unacceptable status quo, and of risking the institution's academic prestige and standards. Since this is a potentially damaging and divisive issue, the cochairs of the committee have decided to attempt a mediation approach to resolving some of the issues and relieving tensions. Accordingly, the cochairs asked each committee member to name another committee member who best spoke for their interests and concerns and for the institution's interests. The cochairs then recommended that two members representing different perspectives participate in a mediation. The four people—the cochairs, acting as mediators, and the two representatives—will then report back to the full committee.

Background Information

The school of education has an excellent academic reputation. Its faculty have strong research and publication portfolios, and many are involved in educational reform movements in the state and nationally. Of the forty-seven faculty in the school, eleven are women. There is one African American and one Asian American on the faculty. None of the female or minority faculty are full professors. The school's undergraduate student population is 78 percent female. Its graduate student population is 46 percent female. Twelve percent of the students are from ethnic minority groups. The state's minority population is approximately 10 percent.

Advocate for Increasing Diversity Role

You believe the accreditation team is right on target—the institution and the school have dragged their feet on the diversity issue. The patterns of institutionalized racism and sexism are clear. You know it firsthand. It's a smoke screen to say that those who favor change are engaging in race-based politics, don't care about standards, or care only about political correctness. This fight is about fairness and being actively opposed to bias and prejudice. You want criteria that will bring women and minorities into the pool, get them in the door, and give them a chance to compete in a fair game.

Mediation: Faculty Personnel Committee (Advocate for Maintaining Current Standards Role) _____

Situation Summary

A recent accreditation report recommended that your institution take steps to provide greater diversity on its faculty. The school of education was specifically mentioned as needing policies to improve the recruitment and hiring of qualified faculty from under-represented groups. The dean has asked the personnel committee to draft guidelines for these policies quickly, since a search must be begun ASAP for a tenure-track position. The personnel committee has had one meeting. That meeting ended badly. The committee was split around the question of selection standards. Members accused each other of racism, of favoring race over credentials and competency, of protecting an unacceptable status quo, and of risking the institution's academic prestige and standards. Since this is a potentially damaging and divisive issue, the cochairs of the committee have decided to attempt a mediation approach to resolving some of the issues and relieving tensions. Accordingly, the cochairs asked each committee member to name another committee member who best spoke for their interests and concerns and for the institution's interests. The cochairs then recommended that two members representing different perspectives participate in a mediation. The four people—the cochairs, acting as mediators, and the two representatives—will then report back to the full committee.

Background Information

The school of education has an excellent academic reputation. Its faculty have strong research and publication portfolios, and many are involved in educational reform movements in the state and nationally. Of the forty-seven faculty in the school, eleven are women. There is one African American and one Asian American on the faculty. None of the female or minority faculty are full professors. The school's undergraduate student population is 78 percent female. Its graduate student population is 46 percent female. Twelve percent of the students are from ethnic minority groups. The state's minority population is approximately 10 percent.

Advocate for Maintaining Current Standards Role

The accreditation team didn't address the problem of recruiting qualified minority candidates in a state with a low minority population. There are few outstanding candidates whose academic record would fit the school's needs. Competition for those few is stiff. You regret that societal conditions limit the academic opportunities of women and minorities. Something should be done to encourage women and minorities to go to graduate school and seek academic careers, but the school can't risk its reputation by lowering standards to bring in lesser-qualified candidates. It wouldn't be fair to the candidates, the current faculty, the students, or the school.

Intercultural Case Study _____

This case study provides you with the opportunity to practice problem analysis, negotiation, and collaborative problem solving. You will find below the situation summary, the faculty member role, the principal role, and the student role. We recommend the principal role and the student role for use in a *negotiation* role play. Use any of the roles together for a mediation role play. Use all of the roles for a collaborative problem-solving role play. All role players should receive the situation summary in addition to the role they will play.

Situation Summary

Your school has experienced a recent dramatic shift in student demographics. The number of European American students has decreased by 25 percent, and the number of African American and Latino students has increased by 30 and 10 percent, respectively. The faculty, predominantly European American, has not changed.

The school is trying to diversify the faculty and increase the number of bilingual teachers and counselors. Tensions are high, however. Several faculty members and students are complaining about the amount of resources being devoted to the new students. Several comments have focused on the need to "get our school back" and the importance of not letting "them" take over. Yesterday, in the faculty cafeteria, a teacher said, "Gee, this used to be such a nice school with a good reputation."

The school has always had its share of student disputes, but the number of disputes has increased in the last few months. Fights have occurred between students of different ethnic backgrounds and among students sharing the same ethnicity. Most of the fights involve two or three students, but the most recent dispute, between European American and African American students, involved nine people. All of the students involved in the fight were suspended, but the European American students received one- or two-day suspensions, while most of the African American students received three- to five-day suspensions.

The school has a peer mediation program. All student disputes that do not involve weapons or serious physical injury are referred to the mediation program for resolution. If the students cannot resolve their differences, then everyone is suspended.

Faculty Member Role

You have a reputation among both students and faculty for being honest and fair. Because they trust you, several students have come to you and complained about unfair treatment in the selection of who gets sent to mediation. They claim that every dispute that involves European American students gets sent to mediation, but when the dispute is between African American or Latino students, they are automatically suspended and are not sent to mediation. The students believe that the only reason the European American students were suspended in the nine-person dispute is because one of the African American students was seriously injured.

Principal Role

You are a European American female. As the principal of Ridge High School, you have had to deal with a number of complex situations. You have always prided yourself on your ability to listen and communicate with parents, teachers, staff, and students. You have been at the school for ten years and have begun to think it is time to move to a different position. But recently a number of unsettling events have taken place at the school, and you really want to attend to them. You don't want to leave the school in a crisis. Most of these recent occurrences have involved complaints about insensitivity to racial, religious, and ethnic differences.

A faculty member at your school met with you yesterday to discuss the situation, in which some students feel that mediation is not being used fairly across the student population. Students of color feel that they are more likely to be suspended after disputes involving European American students and that it is unfair. You pride yourself on fairness and do not feel that your school has a double standard of justice. If a student gets suspended, that is because the offense warrants that response. Also, the mediation program was your baby, reflecting your flexibility and fairness in handling conflicts on campus. However, you are concerned about the misperception of unfairness. Accordingly, you have agreed to meet with a student representative to discuss the concerns of African American and Latino students and to assure these students that all students are treated the same in your school.

Student Role

You are an African American male and a senior at Ridge High. Over the past three years you have noticed a steady increase in racial tensions, which you feel is in direct proportion to the increase in students of color. When you first came to this school, you felt very much like an outsider. You still do, given the makeup of the staff; but at the same time, you have been able to develop more of a feeling of belonging as part of a group of students of color. Last year you got involved in the mediation program because you felt that it would be a good way to deal with some of the things that were happening in the school.

At this point you feel pretty hopeless about things changing. You and some other students met with a faculty member a couple of days ago to complain about the unfair treatment of students of color in the mediation program. The faculty member has spoken to the principal. The principal has requested a meeting with a student representative to discuss the issue, and the other students chose you. You haven't had much contact with the principal, but you know she is very supportive of mediation and in fact was the founder of the school program. You also know that she OK's all suspensions. So you are feeling very apprehensive and cautious about this meeting, and you don't really expect to get anywhere. You can't imagine that the principal will admit to the racism that permeates this school. However, your friends are all counting on you.

Exploring the Dynamics of Power in Conflict Resolution

Susan J. Koch

As everyone with experience in conflict resolution knows, the importance of power—who has it, who does not, and how it affects conflict resolution processes—is one of the fundamental concepts in conflict resolution theory and practice. An awareness of sources of power and the ways in which power impacts conflict resolution processes is crucial for individuals who work as conflict resolution educators, negotiators, and mediators. The purpose of this appendix is to discuss the dynamics of power in conflict resolution processes and to suggest actions that can be taken to reduce the potential negative effects of power on the conflict resolution process.

Understanding the Power in Conflict

Like the word *conflict*, the term *power* usually provokes a number of common associations, such as power plays, power politics, overpowering someone or something, a powerhouse, strong-arm tactics, authority, and influence. Power is often equated with coercion, injustice, and force. Also like *conflict*, these terms express a belief that power is usually negative and often involves one individual's dominating another. Hocker and Wilmot (1991) propose another orientation toward power—power with others. This view is predicated on the following assumptions:

1. Power is present in all interactions.

2. Power is neither positive nor negative; it just is.

3. Power is the product of interpersonal relationships, not of the individuals involved in them.

4. People attempt to balance power, either productively or destructively.

5. Productive power balancing can occur by expanding the sources of power.

6. A relative balance of power is necessary for productive conflict management.

This view, which is more compatible with a view of conflict as an opportunity for growth, contrasts with a finite image of power. Power does not have to be equated with the opportunity to do damage; it can also mean the ability to influence the decisions of others—in ways that are positive for both parties. This view is compatible with what we refer to in conflict resolution as the integrative or win-win approach. When disputants take a win-win approach, they are less likely to use power for the benefit of one and more likely to create ways to satisfy both parties' needs.

Sources of Power

Every individual involved in a conflict has power. But often only the more obvious sources of power—money, large physical size, knowing how to operate a computer, for example—are recognized. One of the key issues for the conflict resolution educator is to be able to recognize all the sources of power and holders of power in a given conflict situation.

To further complicate the issue, a particular source of power equates to *real* power only if others in a given conflict view it as valuable. (For example, someone who is an expert at basketball will probably not be particularly powerful when attempting to join a school band. Being good at basketball is not valued by the band director.) In other words, power is not an attribute that people possess, as in "She is a powerful person." Rather, power is a product of social relationships. Power cannot exist unless someone places a value on a particular attribute.

Conflict researchers classify sources of power in a variety of ways. The following are posited by Mayer (1987):

1. *Formal authority.* Power derived from a formal position (a public office, the role of parent, an administrative position in a school).

2. *Expertise or information-based power.* Power derived from expertise in a particular area or from possessing information that others do not have.

3. *Associational power.* Power derived from association with other people who have power (the boss's friend, the director's golfing buddy).

4. *Resource-based power.* Power derived from control over valued resources like money, materials, and so on; can also be a product of the ability to deny such resources to others.

5. *Procedural power.* Control over the procedures by which decisions are made (school or office secretary, person who makes up a meeting's agenda).

6. *Sanction power.* Power derived from the ability (or perceived ability) to inflict harm or to inhibit another person from realizing his or her interests.

7. *Nuisance power.* Power derived from the ability to cause discomfort; sometimes manifested by verbal, but often by nonverbal, messages of disinterest, disrespect, or disagreement.

8. *Habitual power.* Power derived from the status quo ("We can't change it because things have always been this way").

9. *Moral power.* Power arising from an appeal to widely held values; often results from a conviction that one is right.

10. *Personal power.* Power derived from personal attributes, which frequently magnify other sources of power; marked by self-assurance, determination, endurance, communication skills, and so on.

In most instances, individuals have several of these sources of power at their disposal. The most effective conflict participant is one who has developed several sources of power and becomes skillful at recognizing when to use which one (Hocker & Wilmot, 1991). Additionally, people often link up with others to attain more power by forming coalitions (Van de Vliert, 1981). Anyone who has ever said, "You better not hit me, because if you do, my sister will beat you up" understands the value of coalitions. An important piece of analyzing any conflict is to understand what kinds of power are available to people and which individuals are using various types of power.

Balancing Power

In addition to recognizing sources and holders of various types of power, negotiators and mediators often need to take action to balance power. *A relative balance of power is necessary for productive conflict resolution.*

If the issue of power balance is unrecognized or ignored, progress toward a solution is difficult—the disputants are too busy either trying to hang on to the power they think they have or trying to get more power. People who consistently have higher power risk becoming corrupt, isolated, and self-centered. People who feel powerless tend to resort to apathy, aggression, and violence. In both cases, the resulting activity is not productive for either party or for the process of conflict resolution. Productive and intentional power balancing is usually preferred to the destructive power balancing (shouting, name-calling, sabotaging) that often occurs.

In conflict situations, there are three actions we can take to productively and intentionally balance power: *restraint, empowerment*, and *transcendence.*

Higher-powered parties can *restrain* their power by refusing to use the power source they have. For example, a physically larger teenager may choose not to hit a smaller classmate; the principal may choose not to sentence a student to detention; a parent may choose not to send a child to her room; a teacher may choose not to keep a child in from recess. If these actions had been viewed as expected or typical responses in the past, the restraint demonstrated may change the downward spiral of events that occurred many times in the past.

A higher-powered person can also move to a more dependent relationship with a disputant. This will move the power toward equity and increase the collaborative nature of their interactions. For example, one person in the office might have much greater computer skills, which place her in a high-power position in the eyes of others. The computer expert might ask another staff member to assist her in improving her interviewing skills. She thus becomes dependent on that interview expert.

Empowerment is the second way to balance power. Empowerment is something we can do for ourselves, something we can do for others, or something others can do for us. One way to empower a lower-powered individual is to provide him or her with new expertise, new linkages, or control of more resources. This is, for example, the basis of mentoring—empowering a lower-power person through linkages to persons with higher power. Another way to empower is to create structures in which everyone has the opportunity to be heard. Empowerment also occurs when a third party is invested with the power to intervene on behalf of the less powerful. The mediator, by his or her very presence, often empowers the less powerful, because the process of mediation—if properly managed—ensures that all sides get a fair hearing.

A third way to balance power is to go beyond, or *transcend*, a win-lose structure and agree to work to improve the relationship both before and during the conflict. People can agree (and mediators can suggest) on behaviors that will not be allowed during negotiations (no leaving during a discussion, for example). They can likewise agree that if a serious power imbalance occurs, the high-power person will work actively with the low-power person to alter the balance in a helpful way (or an outside mediator or counselor may be used to achieve this outcome). This transcendence makes it clear that the relationship itself is of primary importance and that the disputants sincerely want to find a solution that is supportive of both.

A positive characteristic of transcendence, commonly observable in strong friendships, is that the person temporarily needy or weaker in the relationship can draw upon or claim extra time, space, money, training, empathy, or other resources with confidence that this action will not only eventually balance the power but also be understood by the other party. This is interpersonal peacemaking at its best.

Whether they exist in a friendship, a family, a school faculty, or an agency staff, power imbalances extending over a long period of time damage relationships and make conflict resolution difficult. An awareness of sources of power, how power affects conflict resolution processes, and ways to balance power are crucial components in conflict resolution training.

References

Hocker, J., & Wilmot, W. (1991). *Interpersonal conflict* (3rd ed.). Dubuque, IA: W. C. Brown.

Mayer, B. (1987, Summer). "The dynamics of power in mediation and negotiation." *Mediation Quarterly*, pp. 296–305.

Van de Vliert, E. (1981, September). "Siding and other reactions to a conflict." *Journal of Conflict Resolution*, pp. 410–418.

Recommended Reading

These reading lists are divided into four areas of interest—conflict resolution, violence prevention, cultural diversity and prejudice reduction, and organizational change and school governance—to assist in selecting materials for personal or classroom use.

Conflict Resolution

Axelrod, R. M. (1984). *The evolution of cooperation.* New York: Basic Books.

Bodine, R. J., Crawford, D., & Schrumpf, F. (1994). *Creating the peaceable school.* Champaign, IL: Research Press.

Bolton, R. (1979). *People skills: How to assert yourself, listen to others, and resolve conflicts.* New York: Simon & Schuster.

Coser, L. (1956). *The functions of social conflict.* New York: Macmillan.

Deutsch, M. (1991). *Educating for a peaceful world.* Amherst, MA: National Association for Mediation in Education.

Deutsch, M. (1986). *Conflict resolution: Theory and practice.* Amherst, MA: National Association for Mediation in Education.

Deutsch, M. (1973). *The resolution of conflict: Constructive and restrictive processes.* New Haven, CT: Yale University Press.

Dewey, J. (1949). *The school and society.* Chicago: University of Chicago Press.

Fisher, R., Ury, W., & Patton, B. (1991). *Getting to yes: Negotiating agreement without giving in (second edition).* New York: Penguin Books.

Girard, K., Rifkin, J., and Townley, A. (1985). *Peaceful persuasion: A guide to creating mediation dispute resolution programs on college campuses.* Washington, DC: National Institute for Dispute Resolution.

Hocker, J., & Wilmot, W. (1991). *Interpersonal conflict* (3rd ed.). Dubuque, IA: W. C. Brown.

Johnson, D. W., & Johnson, R. T. (1989). *Cooperation and competition: Theory and research.* Edina, MN: Interaction Book Company.

Keefe, T., & Roberts, R. (1991). *Realizing peace*. Ames, IA: Iowa State University Press.

Kohn, A. (1986). *No contest: The case against competition*. Boston: Houghton Mifflin.

Kreidler, W. (1984). *Creative conflict resolution: More than 200 activities for keeping peace in the classroom*. Glenview, IL: Scott, Foresman.

Lam, J. (1989). *The impact of conflict resolution programs on schools: A review and synthesis of the evidence*. Amherst, MA: National Association for Mediation in Education.

LeResche, D. (Ed.). (1993). "Native American perspectives on peacemaking." *Mediation Quarterly, 10*(4), 321–432.

Moore, C. (1986). *The mediation process: Practical strategies for resolving conflict*. San Francisco: Jossey-Bass.

Sandole, D. J., & Van der Merwe, H. *Conflict resolution theory and practice: Integration and application*. New York: Manchester University Press.

Schellenberg, J. (1982). *The science of conflict*. New York: Oxford University Press.

Schrumpf, F., Crawford, D. K., & Usadel, H. C. (1991). *Peer mediation: Conflict revolution in schools*. Champaign, IL: Research Press.

Violence Prevention

Creighton, A. & Kivel, P. (1992). *Helping teens stop violence*. Alameda, CA: Hunter House.

Eron, L. D. (1982). "Parent-child interaction, television violence, and aggression in children." *American Psychologist, 37*(2), 197–211.

Eron, L. D. (1980). "Prescription for reduction of aggression." *American Psychologist, 35*(3), 244–252.

Garbarino, J., Dubrow, N., Kostelny, K., & Pardo, C. (1992). *Children in danger: Coping with the consequences of community violence*. San Francisco: Jossey-Bass.

Goldstein, A. P. (Ed.). (1988). *The prepared curriculum: Teaching prosocial competencies*. Champaign, IL: Research Press.

Goldstein, A. P., & Glick, B. (1987). *Aggression replacement training: A comprehensive intervention for aggressive youth*. Champaign, IL: Research Press.

Prothro-Stith, D., & Weissman, M. (1991). *Deadly consequences: How violence is destroying our teenage population and a plan to begin solving the problem*. New York: HarperCollins.

Spergel, I. A. (1991). *Youth gangs: Problems and responses*. Washington, DC: U.S. Department of Justice, Office of Juvenile Justice and Delinquency Prevention.

Vigil, J. D. (1988). *Barrio gangs: Street life and identity in southern California*. Austin, TX: Austin University Press.

Cultural Diversity and Prejudice Reduction

Allport, G. (1979). *The nature of prejudice*. Reading, MA: Addison-Wesley.

Condon, J., & Fathi, Y. (1989). *An introduction to intercultural communication*. New York: Macmillan.

Derman-Sparks, L. (1989). *Anti-bias curriculum tools for empowering young children*. Washington, DC: National Association for the Education of Young Children.

Gabelko, N., & Michaelis, J. *Reducing adolescent prejudice: A handbook*. New York: Teachers College Press.

Gilligan, C. (1982). *In a different voice: Psychological theory and women's development*. Cambridge, MA: Harvard University Press.

Harris, P., & Movan, R. (1989). *Managing cultural differences.* Houston, TX: Gulf Publishing.

Hernandez, H. (1989). *Multicultural education: A teachers guide to content and process.* Columbus, OH: Merrill Publishing.

Jankins, C. (1982). *A look at gayness: An annotated bibliography of gay materials for young people.* Ann Arbor, MI: Kindred Spirit Press.

Katz, J. (1982). *White awareness: Handbook for anti-racism training.* Norman: University of Oklahoma Press.

LeBaron, D. M., Lund, B., & Morris, C. (1994). *Report of the multiculturalism and dispute resolution project.* Victoria, BC: University of Victoria, UVIC Institute for Dispute Resolution.

Renyi, J. (1993). *Going public: Schooling for a diverse democracy.* New York: The New Press.

Samover, L., & Porter, R. (1990). *Intercultural communication: A reader.* Belmont, CA: Wadsworth Publishing.

Tannen, D. (1990). *You just don't understand: Women and men in communication.* New York: William Morrow.

Organizational Change and School Governance

Girard, K., Rifkin, J., & Townley, A. (1985). *Peaceful persuasion: A guide to creating mediation dispute resolution programs on college campuses.* Washington, DC: National Institute for Dispute Resolution.

Murphy, E. C., & Snell, M. (1993). *The genius of Sitting Bull: 13 heroic strategies for today's business leaders.* Englewood Cliffs, NJ: Prentice-Hall.

Poplin, M., & Weeves, J. (1992). *Voices from the inside: A report on schooling from inside the classroom.* Claremont, CA: Claremont Graduate College. (Available from the Institute for Education in Transformation of the Claremont Graduate College. Telephone: 909–621–8287.)

Tichy, N. M. (1983). *Managing strategic change: Technical, political, and cultural dynamics.* New York: Wiley.

Sample Course Outlines

The following outlines illustrate some of the ways material from this manual can be selected and applied, based on the time available and program context. One suggests material that might be used in a short introduction to conflict resolution. The others suggest approaches to a one-credit course or workshop and to a full course on the subject.

One- or Two-Hour Session (Part of Curriculum Methods Course)

I. Presentation

    A. Introductory Ideas About Conflict (Module 1)

        1. There are many definitions of conflict and many associations to the word.

        2. Conflict is not simply about differences, since differences in beliefs, ideas, opinions, and customs may or may not lead to conflict depending on how, when, and where the differences are manifested.

        3. Conflict is neither positive nor negative.

        4. It is important to understand conflict as being organic to the human condition.

        5. We develop habitual responses to conflict, and we must learn new ways of understanding and responding to conflict.

B. Principles of Collaborative Negotiation and Mediation (Module 3)
   1. Negotiation occurs among friends, family members, and associates and within and between organizations.
   2. Negotiation is a step-by-step, unassisted process involving agreement to negotiate, gathering points of view, finding common interests, creating win-win options, evaluating options, and creating an agreement.
   3. There are some conditions, such as motivation to settle a dispute, that favor successful conclusion. Other conditions, such as power imbalances, may impede successful negotiation.
   4. Collaborative negotiation can be extended into a formal, structured process assisted by a third-party.
C. Conflict Resolution Programs in Schools (Module 4)
   1. Programs in schools range from curriculum to peer mediation programs and from student and classroom focuses to staff and schoolwide focuses.
   2. There are three categories of application approaches: in-classroom, school-based peer mediation, and site-based decision making.
   3. Conflict resolution appears in social studies, language arts, citizenship, and health curricula.
   4. In-classroom approaches include integration into the standard curriculum, classroom management style, teaching students how to settle disputes, and violence prevention curricula.
D. Skills of Conflict Resolution (Module 2)
   1. Communication problems include unclear goals, lack of attentiveness, and misunderstandings.
   2. Communication remedies include active listening, focusing on being understood, speaking about oneself, speaking for a purpose, and adjusting for differences of age, sex, culture, and so on.
   3. Communication inhibitors include interrupting, judging, teasing, criticizing, offering advice, changing the subject, dominating the discussion, deception, and refusing to negotiate.

II. Exercises—Communication Skills (Module 2)

A. Exercise 2.2. Taking Stock
B. Exercise 2.10. Improving Communication Using "I" Messages

One-Unit, Fifteen-Hour Course or Workshop in Conflict Resolution _____

I. Nature of Conflict

A. Introductory Ideas About Conflict

1. There are many definitions of conflict and many associations to the word.

2. Conflict is not simply about differences, since differences in beliefs, ideas, opinions, and customs may or may not lead to conflict depending on how, when, and where the differences are manifested.

3. Conflict is neither positive nor negative.

4. It is important to understand conflict as being organic to the human condition.

5. We develop habitual responses to conflict, and we must learn new ways of understanding and responding to conflict.

B. Learning New Ways of Seeing and Understanding Conflict: Looking at Beliefs

1. In any dispute, it is useful to examine the parties' beliefs about what can happen. Some people believe that conflict must result in one side winning and one side losing or that in a conflict situation everybody must compromise; there are other, equally influential beliefs.

2. Beliefs about what can happen in resolving conflicts may be rooted in beliefs and attitudes about relationships, strength of focus on goals, personal characteristics, past experience, comfort with assertiveness and aggression, cultural norms, values, expectations, and so on.

C. Learning New Ways of Seeing and Understanding Conflict: Looking at Stance

1. Examine what the parties say they want. For example, are the parties taking positions? Are they focusing on a specific concrete outcome? Are they able to identify their interests and the broader goals that each side is trying to achieve?

2. Examine the extent to which the parties seem aware of their needs and the cultural factors influencing the conflict.

3. Stress that a satisfying resolution is more likely when

   • The people involved understand that underlying needs must be addressed.

   • Everyone's interests are explored.

- Positions are distinguished from interests.
- Interests are defined, not assumed.
- Interests, rather than positions, are the focus of discussion.
- Conflicting interests are seen as a shared problem to be solved.
- Cultural differences are recognized and understood.

   D. Exercises (Module 1)
      1. Exercise 1.2. Conflict Metaphors
      2. Exercise 1.5. The Beautiful Butterfly Case

II. Foundational Orientations and Skills

   A. Cultural Sensitivity
      1. Cultural factors play an important role in how conflicts are experienced and resolved.
      2. The interplay of cultural factors can be experienced within an individual and between individuals. The culture of the setting in which a conflict occurs or is being resolved can also be a factor in the dynamics of conflict resolution.
      3. While some conflicts are intercultural, all conflicts involve cultural differences.
      4. The ability to recognize and understand the effect of cultural differences is important in the successful resolution of conflict.
      5. Communication skills are a link in the process of being able to hear and understand amid cultural differences.

   B. Communication Skills in Conflict Resolution
      1. Communication problems include unclear goals, lack of attentiveness, and misunderstanding.
      2. Communication remedies include active listening, focusing on being understood, speaking about oneself, speaking for a purpose, and adjusting for differences of age, gender, culture, and so on.
      3. Communication inhibitors include interrupting, judging, teasing, criticizing, offering advice, changing the subject, dominating the discussion, deceiving, and refusing to negotiate.

   C. Lateral Thinking Skills to Aid Conflict Resolution
      1. Lateral thinking includes considering options, generating more ideas, imagining consequences and outcomes, and creating unique solutions.

2. Lateral thinking strategies include brainstorming, changing one's perspective on the problem and its scope, searching for mutual gains, and evaluating options from the other's point of view.

D. Exercises (Module 2)
1. Exercise 2.2. Taking Stock
2. Exercise 2.5. Culture and Conflict
3. Exercise 2.6. Active Listening Techniques
4. Exercise 2.9. Reframing
5. Exercise 2.10. Improving Communication Using "I" Messages
6. Exercise 2.13. Problem-Solving Challenges

III. Conflict Resolution Processes

A. Collaborative Negotiation
1. Negotiation occurs among friends, family members, and associates and within and between organizations.
2. Negotiation is a step-by-step, unassisted process involving agreeing to negotiate, gathering points of view, finding common interests, creating win-win options, evaluating options, and creating an agreement.
3. There are some conditions, such as motivation to settle a dispute, that favor successful conclusion. Other conditions, such as power imbalances, may impede successful negotiation.
4. Steps in the collaborative negotiation process include
   - Agreeing to negotiate
   - Gathering points of view
   - Finding common interests
   - Creating win-win options
   - Evaluating options
   - Creating an agreement

B. Exercises
1. Exercise 3.3. Negotiation Simulation
2. Exercise 4.3. Teachable Moments

Three-Unit, Forty-Five-Hour Course on Conflict Resolution in Education

I. Nature of Conflict (Module 1)

A. Exercise 1.3. Words That Mean Conflict
B. Introductory Ideas About Conflict

1. There are many definitions of conflict and many associations to the word.
2. Conflict is not simply about differences, since differences in beliefs, ideas, opinions, and customs may or may not lead to conflict, depending on how, when, and where the differences are manifested.
3. Conflict is neither positive nor negative.
4. It is important to understand conflict as being organic to the human condition.
5. We develop habitual responses to conflict, and we must learn new ways of understanding and responding to conflict.

C. Exercises
1. Exercise 1.2. Conflict Metaphors
2. Exercise 1.4. Ways of Analyzing Conflict
3. Exercise 1.6. Conflict Analysis

II. Foundational Orientations and Skills of Conflict Resolution (Module 2)

A. Self-Assessment: Examining Personal Beliefs, Attitudes, and Behaviors
1. Conflict as constructive.
2. Conflicts as problems people are capable of learning to solve on their own.
3. Conflict as a mutual problem to be solved cooperatively.
4. Conflict resolution as a way of enhancing learning and interpersonal relationships.
5. Conflict resolution as peace education and a means of growing peace and nonviolence in our world.
6. Conflict resolution for citizenship in a democratic society.
7. Conflict resolution as a social responsibility that schools and teachers must address.
8. Conflict resolution as a part of classroom methods, course curricula, and schoolwide climate.
9. Conflict resolution as a means to creating peaceful school environments through experiences in cooperative learning, structured controversy, school mediation, communication skills, nonviolence, compassion, trust, fairness, emotional expression, respect for self and others, and acceptance of cultural differences.

B. Cultural Sensitivity
1. Cultural factors play an important role in how con-

flicts are experienced and resolved.

2. The interplay of cultural factors can be experienced within an individual and between individuals. The culture of the setting in which a conflict occurs or is being resolved can also be a factor in the dynamics of conflict resolution.

3. While some conflicts are intercultural, all conflicts involve cultural differences.

4. The ability to recognize and understand the effect of cultural differences is important in the successful resolution of conflict.

5. Communication skills are a link in the process of being able to hear and understand amid cultural differences.

C. Communication Skills in Conflict Resolution

1. Communication problems include unclear goals, lack of attentiveness, and misunderstanding.

2. Communication remedies include active listening, focusing on being understood, speaking about oneself, speaking for a purpose, and adjusting for differences of age, gender, culture, and so on.

3. Communication inhibitors include interrupting, judging, teasing, criticizing, offering advice, changing the subject, dominating the discussion, deceiving, and refusing to negotiate.

D. Exercises

1. Exercise 2.2. Taking Stock
2. Exercise 2.1. Conflict Styles in the Classroom
3. Exercise 2.4. Clarifying Orientations Toward Conflict Resolution
4. Exercise 2.5. Culture and Conflict
5. Exercise 2.6. Active Listening Techniques
6. Exercise 2.7. Clarifying Meaning with Open-Ended Questions
7. Exercise 2.8. Summarizing
8. Exercise 2.9. Reframing
9. Exercise 2.10. Improving Communication Using "I" Messages
10. Exercise 2.11. Analyzing Anger
11. Exercise 2.13. Problem-Solving Challenges

III. Conflict Resolution Processes (Module 3)

A. Approaches to Conflict Resolution

1. Negotiation, conciliation, mediation, fact-finding,

       arbitration.

    2. Approaches are differentiated by use of third parties, the specific interests represented, who has control over resolution, and formal versus informal or structured versus unstructured proceedings.

  B. Collaborative Negotiation

    1. Negotiation occurs among friends, family members, and associates and within and between organizations.

    2. Negotiation is a step-by-step, unassisted process involving agreeing to negotiate, gathering points of view, finding common interests, creating win-win options, evaluating options, and creating an agreement.

    3. There are preconditions, such as motivation to settle a dispute, that favor successful conclusion and preconditions, such as power imbalances, that may impede successful negotiation.

  C. Exercises

    1. Exercise 3.1. Beautiful Butterfly Case Revisited

    2. Exercise 3.3. Negotiation Simulation

    3. Exercise 3.4. Informal Mediation

    4. Exercise 3.6. Mediation Simulation

    5. Exercise 2.3. Responding to Conflict

IV. Developing Rationales and Applications for Conflict Resolution in Education (Module 4)

  A. The Emergence of Conflict Resolution Programs in the Schools

    1. Many of the school-based programs of the 1970s grew out of increasing concern over violence in the schools.

    2. Now there are over six thousand programs, with over 300,000 students trained in basic techniques of collaborative negotiation. A few states now mandate such training as part of the approved curriculum.

    3. Programs in schools range from curriculum to peer mediation programs and from student and classroom focuses to staff and schoolwide focuses.

    4. Conflict resolution appears in social studies, language arts, citizenship, and health curricula, in classroom management approaches, and in counseling programs.

  B. Nine Areas Where Conflict Resolution Links to Education

    1. *Education for Democracy.* Conflict resolution can be seen as providing both the skills and the support

required for democratic participation, and the experiences of productive conflict that build a cohesive social fabric.

2. *Progressive Education.* Conflict resolution strategies reflect the principles of progressive education, emphasizing the classroom as a community. Teaching them in school furthers the goal of training students for membership in a fair and harmonious community.

3. *Cooperative Learning.* Conflict resolution teaches skills, such as interpersonal communication, accountability, and analysis, that are an important part of cooperative learning.

4. *Education in a Multicultural Society.* While conflict resolution does not address all the complex issues arising from a multicultural society, it does offer skills and frameworks for handling differences in ways that may lead to improved communications, greater understanding, and less fear.

5. *Multicultural Education.* Awareness of one's own and others' cultures and how culture affects norms, values, and behavior is important in both conflict resolution and multicultural education. Conflict resolution offers practice in skills that are basic to the goals of multicultural education, while multicultural education teaches the awareness and sensitivity needed for effective conflict resolution.

6. *Constructive Responses to Patterns of Injustice.* Conflict resolution processes can provide both a communication framework and an outlet for discussing the prejudice that many students experience.

7. *Violence Prevention.* Conflict resolution provides ways of seeing and responding to conflicts with peers that can lead to empowerment and confidence without violence. Evidence suggests that conflict resolution programs may be associated with decreases in aggression and suspensions for fighting.

8. *Critical Thinking.* Conflict resolution involves developing and applying all the skills of critical thinking to students' concrete experiences, and approaches such as "constructive controversy" demonstrate how elements of conflict resolution can be integrated with critical thinking in many ways.

9. *Site-based Management.* Conflict resolution offers a shared framework for those involved in moving to site-based management, including practical skills not

only for managing conflicts but also for improving decision making.

C. Exercises
1. Exercise 4.1. Conflict Resolution in the Schools
2. Exercise 4.3. Teachable Moments
3. Exercise 4.2. Building Rationales for Conflict Resolution
4. Exercise 4.4. Planning for Implementation of Conflict Resolution by Pre-service Education Students

INDEX

A

Active listening: for conflict resolution, 37, 55–57; in courses, 179, 181

Allport, G., 173

Alternative dispute resolution: analysis of processes for, 77–107; conceptual background on, 78–79; consensus building for, 87–88, 104–107; exercises for, 88–107; mediation for, 83–87, 96–103; module objectives on, 78; negotiation for, 79–83, 93–95; references on, 88; role plays for, 140–166

Anaheim, and multiculturalism, 114

Anger: and conflict resolution, 39–40, 67–69; in courses, 181

Arbitration, defined, 79

Association for Supervision and Curriculum Development, 32

Attitudes: on conflict, 6–8, 16, 17, 23; and conflict resolution, 31–35, 46–52; in courses, 176, 177, 179, 180, 181

Augsberger, D., 30–31, 41

Axelrod, R. M., 172

B

Beautiful Butterfly Case: for alternative dispute resolution, 89; conflict in, 18–20; in courses, 178, 182

Beliefs. *See* Attitudes

Blue Line Exercise, 70–71

Bodine, R. J., 33, 36, 41, 80, 88, 172

Bolton, R., 38, 41, 172

Brainstorming, for conflict resolution, 40, 74–76

Butterflies. *See* Beautiful Butterfly Case

C

Camels Exercise, 72

Carlsson-Paige, N., 117–118, 125

Carnegie Council on Adolescent Development, 117, 125

Center for Teaching Peace, 32

Chicago, and multiculturalism, 114

Children's Creative Response to Conflict Program, 111

Children's Project for Friends, 111

Classroom management, and educational applications, 120, 122

Collaboration, in negotiation, 79–83, 93–95

Communication skills: checklist on, 57; and conflict resolution, 36–38, 55–66; in courses, 176, 178, 179, 181; in negotiation, 82–83

Community School Movement, 31

Conciliation, defined, 78

Condon, J., 173

Confidentiality, in mediation, 85

Conflict: analysis of nature of, 1–25; analyzing, 15–17, 21–24, 184; beliefs on, 6–8, 16, 17, 23; categories of, 5; conceptual background on, 2–10; and cultural characteristics, 3–4, 7, 9; defining, 2, 12–14; and developmental needs, 9–10; discussion guide on, 22–24; exercises on, 11–25; focusing questions on, 17; and interests, 8, 18–20; metaphors of, 13, 178, 180; module objectives for, 1; nature of, in courses, 175, 177–178, 179–180; and needs, 8–9, 18–20; origins of, 3–4, 15, 17, 22; positions in, 8, 18–20; principles of, 1; references on, 10–11; responses to, 44–45, 48–49, 186; sculpture of, 25; sources of, 4–5, 15–16, 17, 22; and stance, 8–10, 16, 17, 23–24; styles of, 43–49, 185; types of, 5–6, 16, 17, 22–23; words meaning, 14

Conflict Attitudes Assessment, 30

Conflict Mode Instrument, 29–30

Conflict resolution: active listening for, 37, 55–57, 179, 181; alternative dispute resolution processes for, 77–107; analysis of skills for, 27–76; and anger, 39–40, 67–69, 185; and attitudes, 31–35, 46–52; brainstorming for, 40, 74–76; and communication skills, 36–38, 55–66; conceptual background on, 28; courses on, 125; and cultural sensitivity, 35–36, 37–38, 53–54; educational applications of, 109–133; and emotions, 38–40, 67–69; exercises on, 42–76; glossary on, 135–139; I statements for, 37, 65–66, 176, 179, 181; lateral thinking for, 40–41, 70–76, 178–179; meaning clarification for, 58–59, 181; module objectives for, 27; power dynamics in, 167–171; reasons for, in schools, 127–129, 182–184; references on, 41–42, 172–173; reframing for, 61–64, 179, 181; and self-assessment, 28–31, 39, 43–49, 180; skills for, in courses, 176, 180–181; steps in, 179, 181–182; summarizing for, 60, 181

Conflict Resolution in Teacher Education Project, 124–125

Conflict Styles Instrument, 30

Consensus, defined, 87

Consensus building: for alternative dispute resolution, 87–88, 104–107; educational applications of, 121; steps in, 105, 107

Coser, L., 175

Crawford, D., 5, 11, 33, 36, 41, 57*n*, 80, 84, 88, 172, 173

Creighton, A., 92*n*, 120, 125, 173

Critical thinking, and education, 118, 183